The
CASE
FOR
GOD

To my wife Nathalie, and our children
Ari and Beth
with love

and

To Dr. John B. Cobb, Jr.
in appreciation

The CASE FOR GOD

William E. Kaufman

Chalice Press
St. Louis, Missouri

Excerpts from *Process and Reality by* Alfred North Whitehead. Corrected Edition edited by David Ray Griffin and Donald W. Sherburne, reprinted with permission of Macmillan Publishing Company. Copyright 1929 by Macmillan Publishing Company, renewed © 1957 by Evelyn Whitehead. Copyright © 1978 by The Free Press, A division of Macmillan, Inc.

Excerpts from *Religion in the Making* by Alfred North Whitehead reprinted with permission of Macmillan Publishing Company. Copyright 1926 by Macmillan Publishing Company, renewed 1954 by Evelyn Whitehead.

Library of Congress Cataloging-in-Publication Data

Kaufman, William E.
The case for God / by William E. Kaufman.
   1. God (Judaism)   2. God—Proof.   3. Process theology.
   I. Title.
BM610.K39   1991   211   91-25309
ISBN 0-8272-0458-2

Contents

Foreword

John B. Cobb, Jr.

Ideas, especially philosophical ideas, are often treated in separation from life. When one tells one's story, one usually minimizes the intellectual side. Abstract ideas often get in the way of seeing things as they are, or they provide an excuse for not being honest about feelings and for avoiding decisions. As a result, when people really want to get to know us, they often ask us not to talk about our beliefs.

But, of course, that is a mistake. What we think about our world is a large part of what we are. Sometimes this thinking is barely conscious, little more than an assimilation of the ideas current among our friends and associates. But for others the struggle with belief is fully conscious and articulate. Rabbi Kaufman is one of these others.

What he offers us in these chapters is himself. That is, it is his story as a human being. But in his case, the story is one of struggle with ideas, a struggle for a way of orienting himself in the contemporary world that makes sense. To make sense it must fit with the best thinking and most reliable knowledge of our time. But to make sense it must also give meaning and direction to life and illumine the range of life experience.

In his quest for a way of thinking that makes sense, Kaufman explored several of the most widespread and influential philosophies and worldviews of our time. Of course, in another context he could provide his readers with a much more detailed and rigorous account and criticism, the sort that philosophers offer about other philosophers. But that is not what this book is about. Here we are drawn into consideration of these ideas in a profoundly human way. Do they make sense? Even readers who have never studied philosophy at all will be able to follow much of Kaufman's pilgrimage. And in the process they will learn a great deal about the philosophical climate of the late twentieth century.

Kaufman does not write as one whose quest and search is over. Yet he *has* found encouragement and promise in process thought. He helps the reader see the place of this in the contemporary spectrum and how it makes sense. As another who has found sense in process thought, I can only rejoice.

This book is a new genre. It invites the reader to engage ideas—sometimes difficult ideas—without ever leaving the context of life experience. It begins the process of returning philosophy from its academic seclusion to its humanistic and simply human task. It helps us to see that we are all philosophers whether we want to be or not, and it suggests the line of critical questioning most important for our becoming better philosophers.

Christianity centers on a Jewish savior. Its sacred scriptures are a primarily Jewish book. But the Jewish contribution to Christians did not end there. Time after time, later Jews have contributed to Christian thinking. In our generation, one thinks of Martin Buber, Abraham Heschel, Elie Wiesel, and Harold Kushner, to name only a few who have evoked deep response from Christians. By sharing with us his personal odyssey, William Kaufman may be another. The opportunity for us to learn is there. May there be wide response!

1

The
Crisis
of
Belief

There is a craving for belief in God in our world today. The searching individual often experiences a longing to believe in God for the emotional comfort it offers, but at the same time we do not wish to delude ourselves, even in extreme need. As we strive to believe, there is a gnawing doubt in the back of the mind: Perhaps this is wishful thinking, a fantasy, an illusion. Surely, one thinks, I want to believe, but do I have good reasons for holding this belief?

This book is not an apologia for religious belief. It is, rather, an examination of the case for God as well as arguments against the existence of a deity. The strengths and weaknesses of both theistic and atheistic worldviews

1

will be explored. Specifically, we shall investigate the revisionary concepts of God of religious naturalism and process theology as theological responses to the nonbeliever. In effect, the religious naturalist and the process theologian respond to the nonbeliever that they also don't believe in the existence of an omnipotent creator of the universe, but maintain that this is not what they mean by "God." What do these thinkers mean by "God"? Are their ideas of God coherent and cogent, and can they stand up better under philosophical scrutiny than the traditional concept? These are the questions to be examined in this volume.

This book is addressed to those who are searching or are simply curious about belief in God but who have doubts about the credibility of belief in the traditional notion of God as the omnipotent Supreme Being. It is not difficult to trace the process of attenuation of traditional theological belief in our time. Modern science, beginning with Copernicus, showed that the earth was no longer the center of the universe and that human life is a mere speck in an infinite cosmos. In the light of this cosmic perspective, it appears to be sheer parochialism to insist that the human being is God's special instrument in the scheme of things. Darwin, in his theory of evolution, undermined the possibility of belief in the literal meaning of the biblical account of creation, showing humankind to be the culmination of millions of years of evolutionary development rather than an object of special divine creation. As science revealed more and more laws of nature, it became increasingly difficult to give credence to the accounts of the miracles of the Bible, which implied suspension of these natural laws.

Furthermore, as the social sciences—such as anthropology and sociology—showed the dependence of ancient belief systems on the cultural context of civilizations of their time, it became more and more difficult to accept the notion that any religion could be the product of an infallible divine revelation. For many individuals, then, science seems to rule out the possibility of God's intervention in the scheme of things.

Even more devastating than the challenge of science is the hideous human evil manifested in the twentieth century, epitomized by the Nazi Holocaust. The existence of a morally perfect, omnipotent God seems to be irreconcilable with the monstrous human evil tolerated by such a deity.

Now, one may either confront or try to escape from these facts. The fundamentalist Christian and the Orthodox Jew posit a mysterious hidden divine harmony, holding that these facts, though apparent, are not the whole truth. Despite the prevalence of these attitudes in today's world, I see innumerable individuals who wish to confront the empirical facts, who refuse to accept a fundamentalist faith but are nevertheless searching for a tenable religious world-picture. In this book, the religious world-pictures of theistic naturalism and process theology are contrasted with atheistic worldviews to determine the strengths and weaknesses of each. The point of view of this study is rationalistic, in the sense defined by philosopher Morris Cohen:

> We cannot by the will to believe in a personal God make Him come into existence. We cannot by believing it even add a cubit unto our own stature. Reason in the form of logical science is an effort to determine the weight of evidence.[1]

So the question confronts us: Does the weight of evidence point to the existence of a personal God, an impersonal or supra-personal cosmic divine force, or no deity at all?

Now, no individual can survey the entire universe and determine whether the weight of evidence points to the existence of a deity. No one is in the privileged position to issue judgments of probability concerning what the entire universe points to, for the decisive reason that no one has experiences of universes. "Universes," as C.S. Peirce remarked, "are not as plentiful as blackberries."[2] What we can examine are world-pictures: conceptual frameworks, ways of construing events.

Therefore, the way for thinking individuals to proceed theologically is to examine the weight of evidence in our experience, reading, and thought, in order to determine the world-picture that seems most consistent, is adequate to the facts and basic insights as we see them, and is pragmatically relevant. Hence, theology is to a certain extent autobiographical. As one theologian has expressed it, "every theologian has a story to tell. Good theology is always *embodied* theology. It arises out of and reflects life."[3]

A dominant motif in my life—and, as I suspect, in many lives, especially those of clergy—is the conflict of skepticism with faith. Goethe once said that "the deepest, the only theme of human history, compared to which all others are of subordinate importance, is the conflict of skepticism with faith."[4] This book, an expression of my own inner conflict, is written for those who have had similar experiences. I hope that the insights I have discovered in my spiritual journey may illumine the quest of others who have traversed a similar path.

A Letter from a Scientist

I am both an ordained rabbi and a trained philosopher. In both of these roles, I deal frequently with doubts: my own and those of nonbelievers. When I lead a congregation in prayer, or when I myself attempt to pray, the gnawing doubt is forever lurking that perhaps I am merely talking to myself. These doubts are brought out into the open when I am challenged by a nonbeliever.

Such a nonbeliever is Mort Shor, a scientist who adamantly rejects any form of theistic belief. In a letter to me, he responded to the frequent appeals of fundamentalist preachers to accept the existence of God on the basis of faith:

> The same test of rationality must be applied to all concepts. One cannot have a separate compartment of the mind which deals with faith. I am somewhat disturbed by the assertion that while the

existence of the deity cannot be proved, it also cannot be disproved. We also cannot disprove the possibility of the existence of angels with halos and wings, of Heaven and Hell in the medieval sense of these concepts.[5]

The points Shor is raising are important. Is the belief in God simply a hangover from the primitive beliefs of our ancestors? Is the question of God in the same category as the existence of angels and devils? What happens when we apply the test of rationality to the concept of God?

Being a rationalist myself, I resonated to the challenge of applying the test of rationality to belief in God. Nevertheless, I could not agree with Shor's cavalier dismissal of faith, since faith, although not probative, is a datum that requires examination. What I did agree with was the need to determine whether there are rational grounds for belief in a concept of God that can counteract the considerations that have led to the crisis of belief in our time. My initial response, however, was to reflect on my own personal crisis of belief and its effect on my own religious development.

The Echoes in Myself

As I examined my religious beliefs, I realized that the scientist's challenge did not represent anything new. I too had asked these questions; I too had voiced these doubts. The scientist's challenge stirred reverberations of memory within me.

The crucial event was the shattering of my naive childhood faith, the collapse of my belief in the "picture" of God as a cosmic bookkeeper. By a "picture" I mean a worldview, a way of construing events, a framework for understanding and interpreting life. My spiritual autobiography consists of a succession of these pictures. The earliest picture in my life, and the most pervasive in Judaism, is precisely this notion of God as a cosmic bookkeeper.

As children, we learn to think about God and talk about God from religious traditions. In Judaism, the most familiar part of the tradition is embodied in the *Mahzor* or "High Holy Day" prayer book. These holiest days of the Jewish year are *Rosh Hashanah* (the New Year) and *Yom Kippur* (the Day of Atonement). These days are known as Days of Awe or Days of Judgment. God is "pictured" in the High Holy Day liturgy as the Supreme Judge. Like a shepherd who gathers his flock, bringing them under his staff, God is depicted as bringing every human being for review, determining the life and destiny of every creature. According to the Jewish tradition, on Rosh Hashanah "it is inscribed" and on Yom Kippur "it is sealed"—"who shall live and who shall die...who shall be at ease and who shall be afflicted, who shall be brought low and who shall be exalted. But repentance, prayer and righteousness avert the severe decree."[6] In Judaism, as in Christianity, God is portrayed as the cosmic bookkeeper, keeping a record of virtues and sins. Judaism offers repentance, prayer, and righteousness as ways of attaining God's forgiveness. In Christianity, Christ offers vicarious atonement and salvation from sin to the faithful Christian. Divine judgment and retribution for the unrepentant sinner—these are the motifs of Western religion.

This entire world-picture collapsed for me when my mother, Betty, an extremely pious woman, died of cancer at the age of fifty-two. Watching her waste away during those final months filled me with anger against the alleged justice of the divine decree. One particular phase of her tragic last months is indelibly inscribed in my memory. She tried to put on her glasses to read and recite a traditional Jewish prayer called "Ashre." Ashre means "happy"; the prayer begins with the words, "Happy are those who dwell in Thy house; they will ever be praising Thee."[7] Unfortunately, my mother's face was so shrunken because of the cancer that the glasses kept falling from her face. Unable to contain my rage, I left her bedside and went into my room. I took a prayer book, opened to the page of the Ashre prayer, and, weeping in anguish, ripped up the prayer book.

The tearing of the prayer book represented a rupture in my life of faith. Never again, I thought, would my faith be whole. Never again would I have an implicit, unconditional, totally accepting faith. From that point on, at age twenty, a first-year student in rabbinical school, I would be in search of faith. Could I regain it? Could Humpty Dumpty be put back together again?

How was I able to continue my rabbinical studies after that shattering event? My teachers at the seminary urged me to find consolation in my studies: "Study Talmud; seek comfort in the pages of the Bible and the Midrash," they advised. I was also taught to find consolation in the rituals of Judaism—reciting the mourner's Kaddish, observing the practices of the *Halacha*, the Jewish law. The study and the practice of Judaism were comforting and did help to assuage to some degree the grief. But no one addressed my inner doubts and questions. I was nakedly alone with them, hoping eventually that I would discover a new orientation to faith in general and to the Jewish faith in particular. Because of the pragmatic nature of Judaism, my doubts did not incapacitate my study or practice of the Jewish religion. But the doubts remained underground.

At first, after my mother's death, life did not make sense for me. During the day, I studied the ancient Hebrew texts—Bible, Mishnah, Midrash—but at night I read the writings of skeptical philosophers such as Bertrand Russell, W.V.O. Quine, and the literature and the philosophy of the "absurd": Camus and Sartre spoke to my inner needs at that time. Their writings transcribed my feelings—feelings of anguish, alienation, and rootlessness.

In the following two chapters, I examine the atheistic world-picture of these thinkers—"Atoms and the Void" and the "Absurd." It is my firm belief that to be intellectually honest, one must confront these godless world-pictures, for a faith that does not emerge from the crucible of doubt is not worth having.

Thus, this book is a response to the nonbeliever *within myself.* Doubts cannot be repressed for long. Doubt, moreover, can be therapeutic as well as debilitating, constructive as well as destructive. Judaism, after all, originated from constructive doubts about and the struggle against idolatry. In this book, therefore, my aim is to lay all the philosophical cards on the table and confront the issue squarely: Can a case for *any* concept of God stand up against relentless philosophical inquiry? If so, are naturalistic concepts more fruitful? And if not, what are the future directions for religious inquiry?

Method

The method I shall employ in this book is the critical examination of worldviews, utilizing the criteria of inner consistency, adequacy to the entire range of human experience, and pragmatic relevance. As I have said, my point of view is rationalistic: I seek to determine the weight of evidence for the world-pictures I have thought about and lived through. This does not imply that I regard religion as a totally rational phenomenon. Any study of religious beliefs must reckon with the nonrational elements in human experience of the divine. One must consider, for example, studies such as that of Rudolf Otto's *The Idea of the Holy,* in which it is argued that "so far are these rational attributes from exhausting the idea of deity, that they in fact imply a nonrational or supra-rational Subject of which they are predicates."[8] Philosophers are quick to point out that religious experiences of the holy, the sacred, and the mysterious do not necessarily imply the existence of the religious object to which they allegedly point. Therefore, part of the philosopher's talk is to examine religious and mystical experiences to determine what, if any, cognitive value they possess. The study of these nonrational data, however, is itself rational, for how can anything be studied and evaluated nonrationally or irrationally? Hence, my concept of rationalism is broad enough in scope to include the study of the phenomenon of faith, experiences of the mysterious, the sacred, the mystical, and the ineffable.

What I am investigating in this book is nicely expressed by process philosopher Charles Hartshorne's claim: "Our knowledge of God is infinitesimal. Nevertheless it is, I am persuaded, the only adequate organizing principle of our life and thought."[9]

Is this so? First, therefore, I examine atheistic worldviews to determine their consistency, their adequacy to our life and thought, and their pragmatic relevance.

A frequent claim of the atheist is that the burden of proof lies with the theist, for it is the theist who allegedly violates the principle known as Occam's Razor—that entities are not to be multiplied unnecessarily. Underlying this claim is the atheist's presumption that the atheistic worldview is clearer, cleaner, simpler, and more adequate to the facts than that of the theist. We shall, therefore, explore it to see if, contrary to Hartshorne's assertion, an atheistic worldview such as scientific materialism or non-theistic existentialism is consistent, can serve as an adequate organizing principle of one's life and thought, and is pragmatically relevant. This is our task in the second and third chapters. Chapter 4 examines the claim of the Jewish religious naturalist Mordecai Kaplan that there are positive dimensions of nature of which the atheist fails to take cognizance. Chapters 5 and 6 discuss the process philosophical theology of Alfred North Whitehead and Charles Hartshorne and its critique of scientific materialism. We shall then be in a position to offer an evaluation of Hartshorne's claim that the idea of God is the only adequate organizing principle of our life and thought.

In the course of this book, we shall analyze specific questions that are put to the theist to determine whether the case for God can withstand the attacks of the atheist and the skeptic. Our specific objective is to determine whether a better case for God can be made for revisionary concepts of the deity, such as those of a limited power, process, or agent, that run counter to the standard conservative notion of God as an omnipotent being. It is this conservative standard concept that has been the target of most atheistic critiques.[10] Revisionary concepts are often dismissed by atheists in a cavalier fashion.[11] In this book, I try to redress the balance. Whether or not these "newer" ideas of God can stand up under scrutiny both *internally*, as legitimate reinterpretations of traditional belief, and *externally*, as judged by philosophical criteria, is what we shall ultimately seek to determine. Are they adequate responses to the nonbeliever? If not, does the debate between theist and atheist issue in a stalemate? Or are either of the atheistic world-pictures persuasive or cogent? We turn now to an examination of an atheistic world-picture: atoms and the void.

Notes

[1] Morris Raphael Cohen, *Reason and Nature*. The Free Press, 1964, p. 21.

[2] Quoted in Antony Flew, *God: A Critical Inquiry*. Open Court Publishing Co., 1984, p. 68.

[3] Richard Rubenstein, *Power Struggle*. Charles Scribner's Sons, 1974, p. 1.

[4] Goethe, *Wisdom and Experience*, translated and edited by Herman J. Weigard. Pantheon Books, 1949, p. 72.

[5] Letter of Mort Shor, January 25, 1985; quoted with permission.

[6] *High Holiday Prayer Book*, edited by Morris Silverman. Prayer Book Press, 1951, p. 148.

[7] *Daily Prayer Book*, translated and edited by Philip Birnbaum. Hebrew Publishing Co., 1977, p. 58.

[8] Rudolf Otto, *The Idea of the Holy*, translated by John W. Harvey. Oxford University Press, 1958, p. 2.

[9] Charles Hartshorne, *The Logic of Perfection*. The Open Court Publishing Co., 1962, p. xix.

[10] See, e.g., Flew, *God: A Critical Inquiry*.

[11] *Ibid.*, p. 11, where Flew dismisses such concepts as "the more way-out, off-beat, individualistic interpretations."

2

Atoms
and
the
Void

After the tragic death of my mother, I was attracted to the worldviews of agnostic and atheistic philosophers. I found Bertrand Russell's world-picture in "A Free Man's Worship" initially compelling:

> That man is the product of causes which had no prevision of the end they were achieving; that his origin, his growth, his hopes and fears, his loves and beliefs, are but the outcome of accidental collocations of atoms; that no fire, no heroism, no intensity of thought and feeling, can preserve an individual life beyond the grave; that all the labors of the ages,

all the devotion, all the inspiration, all the noonday brightness of human genius, are destined to extinction in the vast death of the solar system, and that the whole temple of man's achievement must inevitably be buried beneath the debris of a universe in ruins—all these things, if not quite beyond dispute, are yet so nearly certain that no philosophy which rejects them can hope to stand. Only within the scaffolding of these truths, only on the firm foundation of unyielding despair, can the soul's habitation henceforth be safely built.[1]

Russell's unyielding despair was cleansing and refreshing. Remarkably, I found a strange sort of comfort in it. From a cosmic point of view, we human beings were insignificant, nothing more than "the outcome of accidental collocations of atoms" in a purposeless cosmos, devoid of meaning.

How could I reconcile the attraction of atheism with my deep longing for belief? Perhaps it was a way of containing my rage against the God of traditional belief. Michael Novak, a believer, writes: "There is something compelling in the vision of Prometheus, chained to the rocks, defying the gods. It is satisfying sometimes to rage openly—'Do not go gently into that good night.'"[2] And he adds, "The believer remains in the part of his conscience where belief and unbelief war."[3]

So did belief and unbelief war in my soul: the Jewish belief in the omnipotent will of God versus the attraction to the "desert landscape" of a purposeless cosmos. Another factor intensified my inner conflict. After my mother's death, I grew closer to my father, Harry. The marriage of my parents had been a union of two irreducibly opposed natures. Whereas my mother was a pious believer, adhering rigidly to the rituals of Judaism, my father was an agnostic whose "religion" was literature. An unfulfilled writer, he worked as an engineer in the Philadelphia naval base. But in every spare moment, he was either reading or writing. One of my most indelible childhood memories was returning home after Sabbath services to find my father smoking his cigar and typing an article—both activities being forbidden by Jewish law on the Sabbath. My father's wide readings in secular and scientific literature had led him to reject a naive belief in a supernatural deity who "commanded" ritual observance. My mother was, of course, enraged at my father's open disavowal of Jewish religious observance. His retort was that a humanistic ethics was far more important than slavish obedience to ritual. Invariably, he would point to examples of Jews who would adhere to every iota of the ritual law, but in business would employ all sorts of sharp practices to cheat their fellow man. In this stance, my father stood squarely in the tradition of the prophets of Israel who regarded ritual without ethics as hypocrisy.

The conflict between my parents was a major chronic circumstance of my life. Like Goethe's Faust, "two souls dwelled within my breast"—the simple piety of my mother versus the questioning skepticism of my father. My father expired eight years after my mother's death. Their two opposed natures by then were inscribed indelibly in my subconscious mind. My interest in philosophy and theology can in part be attributed to my effort to resolve the conflict between faith and skepticism, which their memories represent. Their memory helped to generate my quest to discover what the Kabbalists—the Jewish mystics—call "the root of my soul": whether, in the depths of my being, it is belief or unbelief that will ultimately be decisive. Thus, I was embarked on the journey to seek the truth. For this reason, my confrontation with atheism is a necessary component of my intellectual and spiritual voyage.

The heart of the matter is Russell's assertion that it is "nearly certain" that human beings are but the product of "accidental collocations of atoms." To investigate this claim, I propose that we explore the world-picture of "atoms and the void" as presented by the influential American philosopher, Willard Van Orman Quine. My interest here is in one aspect of Quine's philosophy: his reasons for rejecting belief in a deity and his "picture" of a world without God.

Quine's Atomistic Materialism

A troubling stumbling block for believers is that many first-class minds get along quite well without a spiritual orientation. Some time ago, I attended a lecture by Quine. After the lecture, I asked him about belief in God. He replied, paraphrasing the French scientist LaPlace, "God is an hypothesis I do not need." What does Quine believe?

Quine provides an account of his beliefs in a symposium entitled "What I Believe." Here he presents his "picture" of the world:

> The world is a multitude of minute twitches in the void. They are microphysical events, related to one another by any three or four forces...everything in the world comes down to elementary particles or microphysical events, whatever one's point of view.[4]

Like those of the ancient atomists—Democritus, Epicurus, and Lucretius—Quine's picture of the world is one of atoms (more precisely, the smallest particles that compose the atom) and the void (space). The ancient atomists did not think it was necessary to account for the origin of this motion of the atoms in space. They thought that the original motion of these atoms was similar to the motion of dust particles as they dart off in all directions in a sunbeam even if there is no wind to impel them. Things as we know them simply originate in the motion of the atoms. Moving in space, the atoms were originally single individual units, but inevitably they began to collide with each other, and in cases where their shapes were such as to permit them to interlock, they began to form clusters. The important point is that the atomists' conception of the nature of things was mechanical: Everything was a product of the collision of atoms moving about in space. Their theory had no place in it for the element of purpose or design. Their materialist reduction of all reality left no place for a creator or designer. They saw no need to account for the origin of the atoms or for the original motion impelling the atoms, since the question of origins could always be asked—even about God. For them, it was sufficient to ascribe eternal existence to the material atoms.⁵

Like the ancient atomists, Quine rejects the notion of a theistic designer. He admits that belief in God is rich in comforts, such as the dream of life after death and a reward for virtue unrewarded on earth. But, Quine asserts, there is no evidence for the truth of theism. He rejects the argument from design, according to which the intricacies of nature bear witness to a cosmic designer. He repudiates this argument because it is not a scientific explanation: "God's *modus operandi* is fully as hard to explain as the intricacies of organic nature."⁶ There is no room in Quine's system for God because the notion of a deity fails as a scientific explanation: It neither explains the past nor allows us to predict the future. Quine does not countenance any alternative avenues of discovery other than science. He concludes that "it can be affirmed with all the confidence of sound scientific judgment that there is no God or afterlife."⁷

How, we might ask, does Quine's materialism account for the human mind and for values? Quine's picture of the world as ultimately consisting of elementary particles or microphysical events applies emphatically to the human mind. He says: "Mind is part of the activity of a physical object, the human animal. Self-awareness is just one of the various perspectives upon a physical object."⁸ But who is doing the looking? Quine sees no reason to impugn psychology, but he holds that psychological explanations of behavior in terms of motive and purpose need not conflict with physical explanations, for "there is no motivation, no purposive action, without neural impulses to initiate it."⁹ Quine thus reduces human behavior to causal chains of elementary physical forces, and the self to a series of microphysical events.

Concerning questions of ethics and the justification of moral values, Quine maintains that the ground of values is utterly human, arising from the need to reconcile the conflicting desires of the members of society. As we would anticipate, he adamantly rejects "the hypothesis of the existence of God as an objective basis for the moral values because what it purports to explain is not a known state of affairs, but only a desired one—namely, the objectivity of moral values."[10] To attempt to ground ethics in the will of God is merely a case of wishful thinking.

Quine is as emphatic a nonbeliever as we will meet. What are the reasons and motives for his unbelief? He sees science as the only route to truth; the idea of God can only be discussed as a scientific hypothesis and, as such, it fails. Quine's motive is his quest for simplicity. He adheres rigidly to "Occam's Razor"—the philosophical principle that entities are not to be multiplied unnecessarily. Quine clearly wants to "shave" the world down to its simplest elements and to clean it up for scientists to do their work without unnecessary presuppositions.

How shall we evaluate Quine's world-picture, utilizing our criteria? According to his premises, Quine's worldview is consistent: It is simple, clear, and precise. But is his worldview adequate? Does it account for all dimensions of existence? One critic nicely characterizes Quine's picture:

> The best way to characterize Quine's worldview is to say that...there is fundamentally only one kind of entity in the world, and that is the kind studied by natural scientists—physical objects; and second, that there is only one kind of knowledge in the world, and it is the kind that natural scientists have.[11]

Quine's materialism thus represents the modern reduction of reality to a single ontological level. Surely, nothing in what science has discovered controverts the existence of aspects of reality beyond the scope of science to discover.

Pragmatically, Quine's analysis is relevant if one accepts his presupposition of simplicity as the criterion for evaluating worldviews. However, another scientifically oriented philosopher, Alfred North Whitehead, has warned us to seek simplicity but also to distrust it. The thick texture of the world, the spiritual depths of human experiences, the tangled web of human emotion all point to the difficulty of explanations reducing complex phenomena to accidental collocations of atoms in the void.

The crux of the matter is whether or not to construe the idea of God as an hypothesis that explains the world. Quine rejects the argument from design because he holds that it fails as an explanation. He would also reject the cosmological argument for an ultimate cause of the universe for the same reason. Our next step is to explore these arguments.

Is God an Explanation? Cosmological and Teleological Arguments

An explanation, in a general sense, refers to the giving of a reason or reasons why something is the case. The statement, "The windows of John's car are closed because he is running his air conditioner," offers an explanation for the windows being closed, namely, the alleged fact that John is running his air conditioner. To verify the explanation, all we have to do is check and see if, in fact, John is running his air conditioner and to ask John whether in fact this is the reason his windows are closed.

A scientific or "hard" explanation involves predictive accuracy and independent testability. It is obvious that religious beliefs do not purport to make accurate predictions about specific events, nor are they independently testable: This is simply not their job. So, by no stretch of the imagination can belief in God be construed as a scientific hypothesis or explanation.

There is, however, a broader "soft" way of construing "explanation." To "explain" implies "making plain or 'intelligible.'" A major claim of the theist is that without belief in God, the world is simply unintelligible: It doesn't make sense. To make good this claim, theists generally rely on two types of arguments: cosmological and teleological.

Cosmological arguments take as their starting point the cosmos or universe. A cosmological argument is one that postulates God as the *ultimate* cause of the universe. Notice I have said *ultimate*, not *first* cause. It is generally recognized that arguments for a *first* cause overlook the distinct possibility that a causal series might be infinite. Hence, sophisticated versions of the cosmological argument are based on the alleged *contingency* or dependent character of the world. A cosmological argument, then, is one that postulates God as the ultimate cause of the universe, a cause outside the universe that is self-existent and self-explanatory, lacking the contingency and corruptibility of things within the universe.

The basic thrust of cosmological arguments is that the universe itself is not self-explanatory; it could not be "just there." The basis of cosmological arguments is the principle of sufficient reason, namely, the concept that there must be an explanation of the existence of any being or of any positive fact whatsoever. Now, everyone will admit that the existence of every finite thing has an explanation: I exist because my parents gave birth to me, for example. The controversial question is whether one can argue from the need for explanation of finite facts to the idea that the universe as a whole—the total collection of all finite facts—requires an explanation.

On this issue, the skeptical eighteenth-century Scottish philosopher, David Hume, in his *Dialogues Concerning Natural Religion,* asked a pointed question: "But can a conclusion, with any propriety, be transferred from parts to whole?"[12] The nub of the skeptic's argument is that the universe may just be a brute fact, and the principle of sufficient reason may simply reflect our own need for explanation and may not be true of the universe as a whole. Thus, a contemporary skeptical philosopher, Antony Flew, maintains the presumption, always subject to correction, "that the universe itself is ultimate; and hence, that whatever science may from time to time hold to be the most fundamental laws of nature must, equally provisionally, be taken as the last words in any series of questions as to why things are as they are. The principles of the world lie themselves inside the world."[13]

The upshot of the matter is that inferences from the universe as a whole to the existence of a deity transcending the universe are leaps into the unknown. Again, C.S.

Peirce's dictum is apropos: "Universes are not as plentiful as blackberries"[14]—that is, to say anything responsible about the universe would imply, impossibly, that we have at our command other universes with which to compare it. Hence, supernaturalist theism—the belief that God is an entity transcending the universe—cannot serve as an explanation of the universe. These considerations, however, do not invalidate naturalistic theism—the belief that "inside" the universe there are aspects of reality that are rendered intelligible by postulating an immanent divine agency.

In fact, process philosopher Alfred North Whitehead agrees with skeptical philosophers that the idea of a deity utterly transcending the universe is a vacuous notion. He explains:

> Any proof which commences with the consideration of the character of the actual world cannot rise above the actuality of this world. It can only discover all the factors disclosed in the world as experienced. In other words, it may discover an immanent God, but not a God wholly transcendent....We know nothing beyond this temporal world and the formative elements that jointly constitute its character.[15]

It is rather Whitehead's thesis that "God is *in* the world, or nowhere, creating continually in us and around us."[16] The issue then becomes whether we need the idea of a God working "within" or "inside" the world to render what we do know about the universe to be intelligible.

Similar considerations concerning the vacuous character of a totally transcendent deity as an explanation apply to teleological arguments (from the Greek *telos*—end or purpose) or arguments from design. A teleological argument sees the complexity and orderliness of the universe—in particular, the adaptation of means to end throughout nature—as requiring explanation in terms of a divine designer or orderer transcending the universe. The presupposition of these types of arguments is the alleged analogy between the adaptations of means to end in nature to the productions of human contrivance, design, thought, wisdom, and intelligence. This is used to show that the Author of nature is somewhat similar to human minds, though possessed of much larger faculties, proportionate to the grandeur of the work that God has executed. To illustrate: We see a house; we know that the bricks were not assembled by chance, but were designed, planned, and executed by an architect; can we not make a similar inference to the universe as a whole?

Once again, the skeptic Hume applies his critical scalpel to this argument, maintaining that we don't know enough about the universe as a whole to assume an analogy between an architect of a house and the alleged Author of the universe. Perhaps the most devastating challenge ever hurled against supernaturalist theism comes from the pen of Hume, invalidating the inference from part to whole: "What particular privilege has this little agitation of the brain which we call thought, that we must then make it the model of the universe?"[17]

The inference from whatever order or design we find in the universe to a transcendent Creator, possessing intellect and will, is thus too weak to serve as an explanation.

How, then, does the "atoms and the void" theorist explain the order that we do find *within* the universe? Isn't the attribution of world-order to chance as preposterous as imagining Shakespeare's works to be the result of random typing by monkeys? The "atoms and the void" theorist attempts to answer the challenge, offering this account:

> However, what cosmology and biology attempt to do is to show how complex natural systems can evolve from disorder as a result of purely natural happenings. The fallout from the chaotic disorder of the Big Bang gradually cools and settles into hydrogen and helium atoms, and forms into stars and galaxies and solar systems and other elements, all rushing apart from each other, until they begin to cave in....The original living molecules

begin to reproduce and to compete for sustenance, and to develop so...as to improve their reproductive chances.[18]

This "atoms and the void" picture of the world, then, involves the evolutionary story of initial random steps being controlled by environments in which they are made and then providing a context for the control of future random steps. Now, the theory of evolution may undermine supernaturalist theism but not necessarily a religious naturalism that integrates evolutionism within its worldview. Whitehead raises an interesting problem about the plausibility of the "atoms and the void" theory:

> I am, as you see, a thorough-going evolutionist. Millions of years ago our earth began to cool off and forms of life began in their simplest aspects. Where did they come from? They must have been inherent in the total scheme of things; must have existed in potentiality in the most minute particles, first of this fiery, and later of this watery and earthly planet.[19]

What the "atoms and the void" theorist cannot explain is the transition from possibility and potentiality to actuality. In contrast to the "atoms and the void" theorist, Whitehead sees the various elements within the world as requiring an immanent divine principle to render intelligible their actuality. Whitehead asserts:

> The order of the world is no accident. There is nothing actual which could be actual without some measure of order...the universe exhibits a creativity with infinite freedom, and a realm of forms with infinite possibilities; but that this creativity and these forms are together impotent to achieve actuality apart from the completed ideal harmony, which is God.[20]

To Whitehead, the order we find in nature cannot be accounted for without the assumption of the existence of God as an immanent "ordering entity," whose "completed ideal harmony" lures the possibilities of the universe toward their actualization.

The "atoms and the void" theorist will dismiss Whitehead's "possibilities" as unnecessary postulations. The issue hinges on whether an organismic world-picture, such as Whitehead's, is more cogent than a purely mechanistic interpretation such as Quine's. This will be the subject of chapter 5.

Conclusion

C.S. Peirce's dictum that "universes are not as plentiful as blackberries" cuts both ways. It shows on the one hand that the theological concept of a supernatural God is vacuous, for after postulating God as such a being as to design and create the universe, "there our knowledge stops."[21] If we can say nothing meaningful about the entire universe, we can surely assert nothing meaningful about a postulated Creator of the universe. But it shows on the other hand that Russell's claim that it is "nearly certain that we are the product of accidental collocations of atoms," and Quine's categorical assertion that "there is no God," also go beyond the evidence.

The issue, therefore, is whether within the universe itself there are factors that require the existence of God working in the world to render them intelligible. The case for God thus requires an examination of those features of human experience and those aspects of nature "inside" the universe that the naturalistic theist sees as pointers to an immanent divine agency.

We have found in this chapter that supernaturalistic theism cannot serve as an explanatory hypothesis for the universe. Moreover, religious accounts of phenomena cannot be classified as scientific explanations because they lack predictive value and cannot be independently tested. Religious ways of looking at the world, however, can be construed as "soft" explanations in the sense of rendering intelligible, for the theist, dimensions of nature and human experience that purely scientific explanations cannot account for adequately.

Religious pictures of the world serve not only to render the world intelligible for the theist; they also give the religious believer an orientation for living, a frame of reference to find meaning or direction. Can such orientations be found? What about those to whom the world does not disclose such a path? The opaqueness of the world, in this respect, has been named by atheistic existentialist writers as "the absurd." The following chapter explores the "encounter with the absurd."

Notes

[1]Bertrand Russell, "A Free Man's Worship," in *Why I Am Not a Christian,* Simon and Schuster, 1957, p. 107.

[2]Michael Novak, *Belief and Unbelief.* The Macmillan Co., 1965, p. 18.

[3]*Ibid.,* p. 20.

[4]W.V. Quine, in Mack Booth, ed., *What I Believe.* Crossroad, 1984, p. 71.

[5]See Samuel E. Stumpf, *Elements of Philosophy: An Introduction.* McGraw-Hill, Inc., 1979, p. 422f.

[6]Booth, p. 73.

[7]*Ibid.,* p. 74.

[8]*Ibid.,* p. 72.

[9]W.V. Quine and J.S. Ullian, *The Web of Belief.* Random House, 1978, p. 113.

[10]Booth, p. 73.

[11]Richard Schuldenfrei, "Quine in Perspective," *The Journal of Philosophy,* Vol. LXIX, No. 1 (January 13, 1972), p. 5.

[12]David Hume, *Dialogues Concerning Natural Religion,* edited with an introduction by Henry D. Aiken. Hafner Publishing Co., 1948, p. 21.

[13]Antony Flew, *God: A Critical Inquiry.* Open Court Publishing Co., 1984, p. 188.

[14]Quoted in *ibid.,* p. 68.

[15]Alfred North Whitehead, *Religion in the Making.* Meridian Books, 1960, pp. 69, 87.

[16]*Dialogues of Alfred North Whitehead,* as recorded by Lucien Price. Little, Brown and Co., 1954, p. 370.

[17]Hume, p. 22.

[18]Anthony O'Hear, *Experience, Explanation and Faith.* Routledge and Kegan Paul, 1984, p. 139f.

[19]*Dialogues of Alfred North Whitehead,* p. 346.

[20]Whitehead, *Religion in the Making,* p. 115.

[21]*Ibid.,* p. 68.

3

Encounter
with
the
Absurd

The death of my parents left me with a feeling of emptiness and metaphysical anguish. Shortly after my father's death, we moved to a small town in Rhode Island where I served as rabbi of the congregation. I was married to a lovely, beautiful woman named Nathalie, our son Ari had just been born, and shortly thereafter our daughter Beth was born. The people in the congregation were quite pleasant and I enjoyed being their rabbi.

Yet, there was still an aching void in my heart. Anchorless and adrift, I asked myself, "Why were my parents cut down in the prime of their lives—my mother at fifty-two, my father at sixty-two?" Moreover, just as I was getting to know

25

my father and to appreciate his brilliant literary mind, he was taken away from me. Outwardly, I conducted services quite efficiently and gave good sermons; the congregation was quite pleased with me. But inwardly, I was full of doubts and questions. My parents' deaths seemed absurd; life seemed to me pointless and without meaning. The world-pictures that most accurately transcribed my feelings at that time were those of the French existentialists Albert Camus and Jean-Paul Sartre.

Camus' Concept of the Absurd

I have always been fascinated by Camus—his mute mother, his depiction of the blazing Algerian sun, his romantic stance of revolt against the world, and his portrait of man and woman as strangers in an absurd universe. What exactly does Camus mean by "the absurd"? What is his picture of the world?

Camus' whole project is to live "without appeal" to a deity, with pure lucidity—by starting and staying with human consciousness of the world. What does our consciousness disclose about our encounter with the world? In his answer to this question, Camus defines his concept of the absurd:

> The world itself is not reasonable, that is all that can be said. But what is absurd is the confrontation of this irrational [fact] and the wild longing for clarity whose call echoes in the human heart.[1]

To understand this passage, imagine a man invited to attend a meeting. The meeting proceeds aimlessly, speeches are made, but nothing definite is proposed about the future project of the organization or the man's role in the organizational scheme. The man, irate and indignant, rises and complains: "Why was I called to this meeting? What did you invite me here for? What is my purpose here? This whole procedure is absurd."

Analogously, for Camus, we were brought into this world. What for? Who has placed us here? Why? We long for clarity about the meaning and purpose of our existence. But the universe is as silent and mysterious as a sphinx; the world offers no clear answer. The infuriating silence of the universe and its irrationality coupled with our longing and hunger for clarity about the purpose of our existence—this clash is "the absurd." Living in a world whose purpose we cannot explain, we feel like a stranger. Camus' world-picture is of a universe suddenly divested of illusions and lights, a place with no familiar landmarks. Suddenly, it is as if we awaken in a place we have never been before, without memory of a lost home or the hope of a promised land. Anchorless, rudderless, and adrift, we experience uncanny feelings of alienation, strangeness, perplexity, anguish, and anxiety. This too is part of the absurd: "This divorce between man and his life, the actor and his setting, is properly the feeling of absurdity."[2]

A human being alone in a strange place: This is Camus' picture of man and woman in the world. If we really encounter the world, without props and illusions, without appeal to a deity, this is the reality Camus claims we will sense. How does one react to such an existence? One possibility is suicide. "There is but one truly philosophical problem," Camus wrote, "and that is suicide. Judging whether life is or is not worth living amounts to answering the fundamental question of philosophy."[3] Everything else is a game. If there is no ultimate or cosmic meaning, why go on living? Yet Camus' message is that we must go on living as an act of revolt and defiance against an absurd universe: "There is no fate that cannot be surmounted by scorn."[4] The human individual, alone and defiant against the background of an indifferent and unfeeling cosmos: This is the universe of Albert Camus.

In evaluating Camus' world-picture of the absurd, let us inquire first concerning its consistency. Camus' stance is in itself self-refuting. If life is absurd, so too is his writing about and description of its absurdity. The minute he puts pen to paper, Camus is affirming meaning and significance. Camus himself recognized this when he wrote:

> From the moment one says all is nonsense, one
> expresses something that has sense. Refusing all

meaning to the world amounts to abolishing all value judgments....In the darkest days of our nihilism, I sought only for reasons to lead beyond the nihilism.[5]

Camus himself realized that a totally self-consistent nihilism—the belief that nothing has ultimate significance—is virtually impossible to sustain. Consider, for example, our everyday discourse. We may experience "the absurd" when we ask, "What will it all mean a hundred years from now?" And we may tend to conclude, "Nothing really matters." But if nothing really matters, then the statement "nothing matters" doesn't matter either. Such rock-bottom meaninglessness is, finally, self-refuting. Camus, in his tacit assumption that the act of metaphysical rebellion against an alleged unfeeling cosmos has meaning, thereby refuses to plunge into the pit of total despair, the abyss of rock-bottom nothingness. Underneath Camus' revolt, then, we see a glimmer of an existential affirmation of life.

Is Camus' worldview adequate? Does it account for all dimensions of human experience? Camus' concept of the absurd presupposes a divorce between persons and nature. In fact, however, we are a part of nature, not something contrasted with it. Our thoughts and bodily movements follow the same laws that describe the motions of the stars and atoms. Furthermore, Camus assumes an unfeeling cosmos. He does not reckon with the process-organismic view that nature is alive, that feeling is an essential and not an accidental component of the cosmos. Of course, this organismic worldview needs to be substantiated by argument, but Camus does not argue against it. He simply assumes without argument a lifeless cosmos apart from humans and the animal kingdom.

Pragmatically, Camus' picture is an important one. The key to Camus' consciousness of absurdity is "his belief that since all men eventually must die, human existence is utterly meaningless."[6] At certain times in our lives, after experiencing the tragic death of a loved one, as in my experience of my parents' deaths, a stance of defiance and rebellion against cosmic injustice is a necessary coping mechanism. But as a daily mode of existence, it is a difficult posture to maintain. Life is a self-renewing process. Nature has equipped human beings with the healing mechanisms to work through our grief.

Nevertheless, Camus does pose a significant challenge to belief in God. He criticizes philosophers such as Kierkegaard and Chestov who admit the phenomenon of the absurd but who then, from this standpoint, posit the necessity for a leap of faith to God. In contrast, Camus' absurd hero admits the irrational and "embraces in a single glance all the data of experience and he is little inclined to leap before knowing. He knows simply that in that alert awareness there is no further place for hope."[7] Camus' concept of lucidity is precisely his refusal to take the leap of faith; he prefers to remain with the awareness of the absurd.

Surely, Camus is correct in his assertion that a consciousness of absurdity is no argument for a leap of faith. It is only a psychological necessity for those who cannot remain with the absurdity, but a psychological necessity does not prove an ontological reality. What can be questioned, however, is whether our immediate awareness of all the data of our experience, at a given point in time, does in fact disclose the full dimension of experience. It is precisely the claim of the process philosopher, to be examined later, that God can be intuited in our immediate experience. God is in the world or nowhere, Whitehead claims. Martin Buber, the Jewish existentialist, also stresses the importance of divine immanence, the belief that God is to be discovered within experience and is not the product of an inference:

> God cannot be inferred in anything—in nature, say, as its author, or in history as its master, or in the subject as the self that is thought in it. Something else is not given and God then elicited from it; but God is the Being that is directly, most nearly, and lastingly, over against us, that may properly only be addressed, not expressed.[8]

The question Camus leaves us with, then, is whether immediate experience discloses the absurd, as he claims, or whether, as Buber and Whitehead maintain, God can be discovered within human experience. We shall analyze this question in chapter 5.

Sartre's Concept of Nausea

A far darker and more sinister picture of absurdity than that of Camus comes to life in the writing of the French existentialist philosopher, Jean-Paul Sartre. During the academic year 1933-34, Sartre studied German phenomenology under Edmund Husserl. The purpose of phenomenology is to study the structure (logos) of human experience (phenomena) without making any judgment about the existence of the objects of consciousness. For example, as a phenomenologist, one could study the primitive's belief in spirits without making any judgment as to whether such spirits actually exist. The existence of spirits is bracketed—that is, put in parentheses or placed in abeyance. One studies the primitive's consciousness.

Whereas Husserl's concern was to describe meanings and structures independent of existence, Sartre, like the German philosopher Martin Heidegger, does not bracket existence. Rather, Sartre uses phenomenology as a method of describing human experience as it presents itself and appears to human consciousness. Sartre utilizes this descriptive method in his novel *Nausea*.

In *Nausea*, the anti-hero Roquentin experiences the absurdity of existence while gazing at the root of a chestnut tree. He is overcome by a strange feeling of nausea, compounded of fear and disgust, at the naked existence of the chestnut tree. He cannot "digest" this experience: He cannot assimilate it with any familiar pattern of meaning. This experience, like Heidegger's clearing in Being, offers a clue to reality: "existence had suddenly unveiled itself."[9] The tree was just there, superfluous, without reason. So was he too, so too are all of us: "We were a heap of living creatures, irritated, embarrassed at ourselves, we hadn't the slightest reason to be there."[10] Overcome by the contingency of existence, Roquentin does not see it as pointing beyond itself to God. On the contrary:

> The essential thing is contingency. I mean that one cannot define existence as necessity. To exist is simply to be there...I believe there are people who have understood this. Only they tried to overcome this contingency by inventing a necessary, causal being. But no necessary being can explain existence....[11]

The essence or nature of the tree can be explained: its dimensions, its growth from the seed, and its structure. But the tree's existence, like the existence of everything, is a surd; it is irrational, just there. And so too are we just there. For Sartre, the atheistic existentialist, human existence precedes human essence: We create our own essence or nature. This is Sartre's definition of existentialism. There is no divine or ultimate essence that creates us. Human existence is utterly absurd; it is a contingency without God. We invent God as a necessary being because we cannot endure the confrontation with the nothingness of naked existence. I am thus alone and radically free. I can depend only upon myself.

Sartre's existentialism is based on his phenomenological description of existence as it appears to human consciousness. The words Sartre puts in the mouth of Roquentin suggest a picture, a way of seeing: "And suddenly, suddenly the veil is torn away, I have understood, I have seen."[12] Roquentin represents Sartre's unique worldview of existence as disgusting and revolting precisely because it is just here, without reason, without meaning, absurd.

Why then does Sartre not take comfort in a God who would alleviate this sense of contingency? What is at the root of the atheistic existentialist's quarrel with God? Sartre's words on this point are significant: "Existentialism is not atheist in the sense that it would exhaust itself in demonstrations of the non-existence of God. It declares rather that even if God existed that it would make no difference from its point of view."[13] What he means is that

I, and I alone, interpret my world. Even if there were a God, he is saying, we wouldn't know God existed. We would still be utterly alone with our beliefs and interpretations and still be radically free. Metaphysical freedom is not a blessing for Sartre; we are, he says, condemned to be free. Sartre wishes there were divine guidance and help; brute existence is sickening, producing nausea. But since we will never know, and because we are left to rely only on our own resources, it would make no difference to us even if God existed.

Clearly, Sartre longs for a God whose necessary existence would explain our contingent existence, a God who would give us a reason for being and would spare us the anguish of determining our own destiny. Sartre is a disappointed rationalist. He wishes that the principle of sufficient reason were true, that there must be a reason for the existence of the world—a God. As one critic has suggested, Sartre "has emphasized the extreme need of the Absolute, without, however, conceding the existence of an Absolute Being as a remedy to this obsession."[14] His refusal of God, like that of Camus, is based on the fact that he cannot see our immediate experience as disclosing the divine and he will not leap to realms beyond our knowledge. Lacking a feeling of certainty about the existence of God, Sartre holds that the concept of God can make no difference in human life because we cannot find help and comfort in a being who may or may not exist.

In the final analysis, for Sartre, we alone interpret our world. Since the issue of God's existence for us depends on how we interpret events, Sartre holds that we cannot find succor or strength in what is merely one interpretation rather than another. Hence, whether God exists makes no difference to us because we are locked into our own subjectivity.

Evaluating Sartre's atheistic existentialist world-picture from the standpoint of consistency, I must first cite a statement that he is reported to have made shortly before his death—which, if accurate, flies in the face of his entire philosophy transcribed in his writings. In a San Antonio newspaper dated May 28, 1932, in a column by Joseph Sobran, I found the following excerpt:

> Jean-Paul Sartre, you'll recall, was France's premier atheist-Marxist-existentialist philosopher until his death two years ago.
>
> Now comes word that shortly before his death he had second thoughts: "I do not feel that I am the product of chance, a speck of dust in the universe, but as someone who was expected, prepared, prefigured. In short, a being whom only a Creator could put here; and this idea of a creating hand refers me to God."[15]

It is hard to believe in the authenticity of this report. Yet, on reading Sartre, one gets the impression that "he protests too much." His atheism is virulent and vehement, especially when compared to the calm, dispassionate atheism of Quine. Furthermore, Sartre is not altogether consistent. He states that "the existentialist finds it extremely embarrassing that God does not exist"[16] as an *a priori* source of value. On the other hand, he asserts that "even if God existed, it would make no difference from its point of view."[17] Is he asserting that, as an ontological fact, God does not exist—which is atheism? Or is he maintaining that we simply don't know whether God "may or may not exist"—which is agnosticism? And if it would "make no difference" if God existed, why then does Sartre find it embarrassing that God does not exist as an objective giver of value? Sartre's discussion on this point seems internally inconsistent and riddled with confusion. Moreover, it is based more on dramatic effect rather than reasoned argument.

From the standpoint of adequacy, Sartre's phenomenological description of human experience is basically his experience or his interpretation of experience dramatized through the character Roquentin in the novel *Nausea*. The problem with the phenomenological method as employed by Sartre is its generalization from one person's experience to the experience of all. One critic of Sartre maintains, quite correctly I think: "Phenomenology, therefore, requires some kind of auto-critique, not unlike the Kantian one: a critique which controls the results of previous descriptions."[18] No one's description of experience is privileged. We are brought back again to the problem of what is disclosed in immediate experience. Sartre and Camus find absurdity; Buber and Whitehead find God.

In fact, Buber reacts to Sartre's atheism in an essay on "Religion and Modern Thinking." Buber cites a characteristically dramatic Sartrean interpretation of Nietzsche's assertion that God is dead. "He is dead, he spoke to us and now is silent, all that we touch now is his corpse."[19] After noting the rather shocking religious insensitivity of the last part of the statement, Buber reacts:

> Let us try to take it seriously, that is, let us ignore what Sartre really meant by it, namely, that man in earlier times believed that he heard God and now is no longer capable of so believing. Let us ask whether it may not be literally true that God formerly spoke to us now and is now silent, and whether this is not to be understood as the Hebrew Bible understands it, namely, that the living God is not only a self-revealing but also a self-concealing God. Let us realize what it means to live in the age of such a concealment, such a divine silence....[20]

Buber goes on to contrast his own view of the divine silence with that of Sartre. Sartre, locked into his own subjectivity, cannot experience the divine because he sees it as an object. Buber, stressing the *relation* of human beings and God as that of the "I" to an Eternal Thou, interprets the divine silence as an eclipse of God due to our present inability to hear the voice, but hopes for a future event when "the word between heaven and earth will again be heard."[21]

Buber's doctrine of the eclipse of God is itself problematic, especially in the light of—or rather, the *darkness* of—the Holocaust. Was God hiding?

What all this points to is the need to reconceptualize what we mean by manifestations of the divine. Today, unlike the ancient world, people who literally hear the voice of God are generally considered lunatics. But just because God no longer speaks in words does not mean that God is not manifested otherwise. It is the task of the naturalistic theologian, which we shall soon explore, to identify what in human experience and nature are to count as manifestations of the divine.

Pragmatically, Sartre dramatizes, perhaps more forcefully than any other writer, what it means to live in a universe without God. It is a universe where we are thrown back entirely on our own resources, and where we experience anguish and "dreadful" freedom. Sartre's worldview is a picture that cannot be ignored. We must continue to wrestle with it in the crucible of our own experience.

Transition

After the death of my father, when I was wrestling with the atheistic existentialist point of view, a remark of my father's sister, Kitty, kindled the hope that perhaps this bleak view of the world was not the whole truth. "You know, William," she said, "there are still some beautiful things in the world."

One can look at a tree and not experience nausea, as did Sartre. There are beautiful things in the world. Is beauty merely in the eye of the beholder, or is there something in the nature of things that is the objective ground of beauty? To the atheistic existentialist, beauty is imposed upon the world through human interpretation. In contrast, to the religious naturalist, beauty is inherent in nature, to be discovered by us, and is one of the aspects of the universe that is a manifestation of God. It is to a consideration of religious naturalism that we now turn.

Notes

[1]Albert Camus, *The Myth of Sisyphus,* tr. by Justin O'Brien. Vintage Books, 1955, p. 16.

[2]*Ibid.,* p. 5.

[3]*Ibid.,* p. 3.

[4]*Ibid.,* p. 90.

[5]Albert Camus, "The Riddle," *Atlantic Monthly,* June 1963, p. 85.

[6]Germaine Brée and Margaret Guiton, *The Age of Fiction: The French Novel from Gide to Camus.* Rutgers University Press, 1957, p. 223.

[7]Camus, *The Myth of Sisyphus,* p. 28.

[8]Martin Buber, *I and Thou,* tr. by Ronald Gregor Smith. Charles Scribner's Sons, 1958, p. 80f.

[9]*The Philosophy of Jean–Paul Sartre,* edited and introduced by Robert Denoon Cumming. The Modern Library, 1966, p. 60.

[10]Jean-Paul Sartre, *Nausea,* tr. by Lloyd Alexander. A New Directions Paperback, 1964, p. 128.

[11]*Ibid.,* p. 131.

[12]*Ibid.,* p. 126.

[13]Jean–Paul Sartre, *Existentialism Is a Humanism,* tr. by Philip Mariet in Walter Kaufmann, ed., *Existentialism from Dostoevsky to Sartre.* Meridian Books, Inc., 1957, p. 311.

[14]Wilfred Desan, *The Tragic Finale: An Essay on the Philosophy of Jean–Paul Sartre.* Harper Torchbook, 1966, p. 179.

[15]*San Antonio Express,* May 28, 1932.

[16]Sartre, *Existentialism Is a Humanism,* p. 294.

[17]*Ibid.,* p. 311.

[18]Desan, *The Tragic Finale,* p. 190.

[19]Sartre, *Situations I* (1947), 153, quoted in Martin Buber, *Eclipse of God.* Harper and Row, 1952, p. 66.

[20]Buber, *Eclipse of God,* p. 66.

[21]*Ibid.,* p. 68.

4

The
Power
That Makes
for Salvation

Late one night, I turned on the television and tuned into a Christian fundamentalist preacher speaking on the promise of salvation, the belief in eternal life. He spoke about God's plan of salvation and the importance of believing in it. What was his argument? His claim was based on his belief that without eternal life, our lives are merely the result of a cosmic throw of the dice. We are, without God's plan, an evolutionary "crap shoot." Without God's gift of eternal life, human existence seems to be riddled with brutal unfairness. Why does one person live to ninety, and another dies as an infant? Why do so many righteous people suffer?

The preacher's argument was faulty. Because we do not find justice here on earth, it does not follow that there is an eternal life where all wrongs will be rectified. But the preacher's understanding of our human need was correct: We all need salvation. But perhaps salvation need not be conceived of as otherworldly. Can we find salvation in *this* life? Are there aspects of cosmic nature and our human nature that, if realized, can help us to attain salvation from evil?

One of the leading contemporary Jewish philosophers, Mordecai M. Kaplan, delineates in his writings a naturalistic concept of salvation. Kaplan was a professor at the Jewish Theological Seminary in New York. When I studied with him there, I had merely an academic acquaintance with him. A few years after the death of my father, however, I had an opportunity to work closely with him and to study his thought intensively.

Kaplan was the founder of Reconstructionism, a movement of thought in contemporary Judaism that emphasizes religious naturalism and religious humanism. The aim of the Reconstructionist movement is to reconstruct or refashion Judaism to meet the needs of the modern Jew. Kaplan's thesis is that Judaism is not merely a religion but the evolving religious civilization of the Jewish people. What is constant in Judaism is the people, not the doctrine. The doctrine, Kaplan maintains, has undergone evolutionary development in the past and should continue to evolve in the present and future in the direction of religious naturalism and humanism. What Kaplan means by religious naturalism and religious humanism is epitomized in his definition of God as "the power that makes for salvation." Let us explore what he meant by this definition.

The Power That Makes for Salvation

When he was eighty-nine years old, Kaplan came to speak at the synagogue in Rhode Island where I served as rabbi. (He died in 1982 at the age of 102.) At eighty-nine, he was still incredibly vital and vigorous; his lecture lasted for more than an hour and was stimulating throughout.

Surely, his theological system worked for him. Perhaps, I thought, it might offer me "salvation" from the atheistic pictures of an absurd universe dramatized by Sartre and Camus and the cold, mechanistic universe of atoms in the void portrayed by Quine and Russell.

However, I was not going to be won over by charisma alone. I wanted to follow Kaplan's arguments carefully. Eventually, I decided to raise a question. "Dr. Kaplan," I asked, "how did you arrive at your definition of God as the power in the universe that makes for salvation?" He answered: "You realize that we are speaking of how persons experience the divine. 'God' means not only the power in the universe that makes for salvation but also the power in ourselves."

Now I understood Kaplan's concept of religious humanism. He did not seek to reach God by denigrating human beings, by seeing the human person as enmeshed and mired in sin. Rather, he emphasized the latent possibilities in human beings, the capacity in individuals to transcend themselves by striving for goodness, truth, and beauty. That very striving, Kaplan underscored, was evidence of a higher power—God—working within human beings in the quest for salvation.

But note: Kaplan is *not* speaking of salvation in a future life. Here Kaplan utilizes his method of reconstructing Judaism. At a specific stage in the history of Jewish civilization, during the rabbinic period of late antiquity and during the Middle Ages, the concept of salvation functioned for the Jew as belief in an afterlife. Kaplan's method is pragmatic or functional; his concern is with how a belief functions in life. He maintains that, with the advent of modernity and the rise of modern science, belief in an afterlife is no longer functional for the Jew. Yet the human urge for salvation remains. Therefore, Kaplan reasons, we must reconstruct the meaning of "salvation." This is precisely what he does. By "the quest for salvation," he means the striving for fulfillment, the feeling we have when we are utilizing our potential, functioning at our best and on the road toward self-realization, when we are creative, loving, and most human. Kaplan was fond of saying that "man is not yet fully human." He believed that God was at work in the universe driving us to a higher stage in our development, toward a creative metamorphosis.

What Kaplan rejected was the traditional understanding of the Jewish faith, which he designated by the rubric "supernaturalism." He repudiated the notion of a supernatural God—that is, of a being who created and transcends nature, who can miraculously intervene in nature and perform miracles such as the splitting of the Red Sea, who chose the Jews as his elect people, and who revealed his will to them in the Torah, which he gave at Mount Sinai. Kaplan's rejection of supernaturalism was epitomized in the Reconstructionist prayer book, in which all references to the Jews as God's chosen people were eliminated. His theological audacity in changing the prayer book led to the burning of this book by a group of Orthodox rabbis in 1945, and to labeling Kaplan as a heretic in Orthodox Jewish circles. Yet the irony of the situation is that many of Kaplan's followers are rabbis serving Conservative and Reconstructionist congregations, and many contemporary Jews, if questioned about their theological beliefs, would subscribe to some form of religious naturalism.

Now, if God is not a supernatural Being who created the universe, what is the world-picture Kaplan is espousing by defining God as "the power that makes for salvation"?

"God," Kaplan wrote, "does not have to mean to us an absolute being who has planned and decreed every twinge of pain, every act of cruelty, every human sin. It is sufficient that God should mean to us the sum of the animating, organizing forces and relationships that are forever making a cosmos out of chaos. This is what we understand by God as the creative life of the universe."[1] And this is what Kaplan means by religious naturalism.

An ambiguity is present throughout Kaplan's theological writings. On the one hand, he repeatedly refers to God as "the Power that makes for salvation." This phrase seems to imply a conception of God as a unitary force that is the source of human fulfillment. On the other hand, in passages such as the one quoted above, he seems to mean by God a plurality of animating and organizing forces and relationships in the universe. Moreover, he emphasizes throughout his writing that God is not an entity but a cosmic process.[2] The term *power* seems to denote the source or energizing ground of this movement. What then gives the divine process or processes its unity? And what exactly is the relationship between God as power and God as process?

A clue to an answer to these pressing questions is given in Kaplan's statement, "Nature is infinite chaos, with all its evils forever being vanquished by creativity which is God as infinite goodness....The power of God is inexhaustible but not infinite."[3]

Kaplan here identifies God with the process of creativity conquering chaos, with the eternal and ongoing active tendency in the universe to bring order out of chaos. This process is unfulfilled without human beings. Our role in the universe is to transform the potentiality of the creative process in the universe into actuality in our lives, through such values as honesty and responsibility. God as the power that makes for salvation or self-fulfillment is the inexhaustible ground or potentiality that generates the process. This process is the ongoing activity of the divine in the universe, which is actualized when we act according to justice and law. Kaplan here has translated the rabbinic concept of the partnership of humans and God into a naturalistic universe of discourse.

Does the identification of God with the process of creativity in the universe provide sufficient unity to render God distinctive and identifiable? Kaplan is anxious to avoid anthropomorphism. For this reason, he does not refer to God as a being or entity but rather as power, creative process, or creativity. But creativity is without character. Whitehead, for example, sees creativity as the eternal activity of the universe, the underlying energy of realization, the drive toward the endless production of new syntheses. Although creativity is the ultimate notion of the highest generality, for Whitehead, it has no character of its own; it is protean. Whitehead did not identify creativity with

God, for he deemed it necessary for God to have a character, and hence to be an actual entity.

The reason that Kaplan does not move in this Whiteheadian direction is that he wants to avoid not only anthropomorphism but reification: He does not wish to identify God as a being or entity of any kind. But then what gives this process its unity or direction? Human beings are actually the apotheosis of the divine cosmic process, for Kaplan. Kaplan's emphasis on the human aspect of the cosmic process shows a clearer indebtedness to John Dewey than to Whitehead. God, for Kaplan, functions as a reservoir and repository of creativity, but it is up to us to utilize the resource properly in order to achieve salvation or self-fulfillment.

The Problem of Prayer

God, for Kaplan, clearly is an impersonal cosmic process. For many years, I found Kaplan's concept of God sufficient. I then rationalized the problem of prayer in this manner:

> How is prayer conceived of according to this view? It has become commonplace, in this connection, to raise the question, How can one pray to a process? This formulation of the question prejudices the issue, for it unduly restricts the meaning of prayer as praying *to* Someone. It would be more in the spirit of Kaplan's approach to speak of praying *with*; that is, the function of prayer would be to open ourselves to the creative process as it functions in nature and in us.[4]

I no longer find this rationalization adequate. To be sure, Kaplan's theology engendered in me an awareness of the positive forces in the universe and in us that can be identified as manifestations of the divine. But the idea of prayer as praying "with" the creative forces now seems to me to be forced. The question thus arises: Can one find in religious naturalism a conception of a God to whom one can pray and still be intellectually honest?

Such a conception can be discovered in the writing of Alfred North Whitehead, as, for example, in his reference to God as "the ideal companion who transmutes what has been lost into a living fact with his own nature."[5] We shall explore Whitehead's conception of God in the following chapter.

The issue of intellectual honesty I consider to be extremely important. Prayer, or any religious act, is a very dubious enterprise unless one believes that there really is a being or entity with whom we can enter into relation. But there is always the danger that one is projecting something into the nature of things that isn't there. Kaplan alerted me to the dangers of anthropomorphism and projection, issues with which I continually struggle. But his conception of God is no longer religiously adequate for me.

Intellectual honesty compels one to ask: Is there a being who is worthy of worship? What I sought for and ultimately did not find in Kaplan's theology was a coherent metaphysics. What I did find there was a dynamic world-picture of creative processes and relations in tension with the chaos and chance in nature. But his world-picture was incomplete. What is the nature of creativity? What is the relationship between possibility and actuality? How should we conceive the relationship between scientific fact and human aspiration?

The years of study of Kaplan's theology led me to the process philosophical theology of Alfred North Whitehead. It is to that system of thought that we shall soon turn.

Conclusion

Mordecai Kaplan taught me the importance of intellectual honesty. Kaplan would not utter any prayer that he did not believe in wholeheartedly. He could not subscribe to the notion that the Jewish people—or any people or group whatsoever—were God's chosen people. He therefore eliminated all references to the notion of the chosen people from the Reconstructionist prayer book.

But Kaplan's theological reconstruction did not go far enough. What about the notion of prayer itself? The Reconstructionist prayer book continues to address God as "Thou." Is this consistent with Kaplan's avowed aim to avoid thinking of God as an entity of any kind, much less a personal being? Kaplan's answer to this problem was to retain the traditional prayer book's reference to God as "Thou" as a concession to traditional modes of language, even though language distorts what Kaplan believed to be the reality—namely, a universe of impersonal forces and relations rendered personal only through our imposition of human meanings. But is this position intellectually coherent?

Kaplan attempts to defend the religious adequacy of his notion of God as the cosmic process that makes for human salvation in this manner:

> Does the awareness of God depend upon our conceiving God as a personal being, or may God be conceived in other ways, and yet be the subject of our awareness, or the object of our worship? In strictly philosophical thought, the very notion of a personal being, especially when not associated with a physical body, is paradoxical. Nothing would, therefore, be lost if we substituted for that notion one of process, which, at least with the aid of science, most of us find quite understandable. Why, then, not conceive God as process rather than as some kind of identifiable entity?[6]

Kaplan here begs the question concerning whether our concept of action is such as to render unintelligible all talk of incorporeal agency. Philosopher Basil Mitchell argues that the possibility of incorporeal agency cannot be ruled out *a priori*.[7] His argument is based on the fact that the language in which we describe actions is logically distinct from that in which we describe physical movements. Such language presupposes a conscious agent with intentions and purposes, which the agent attempts to realize in his or her environment. He adduces as evidence the possibility of telekinesis—the alleged power to alter events such as the fall of dice simply by "willing." Whether or not telekinesis actually occurs, the conditions under which we should be prepared to admit its occurrence can be specified. For example, if the dice were to fall with a certain number upward whenever a particular individual was asked to bring it about and not otherwise, we should conclude that this person had the power to cause physical changes without bodily movement. Similarly, criteria can be specified for an event being caused by an incorporeal agent—namely, the unlikelihood of the event's occurrence apart from the intervention of some agent, the event's contributing to some purpose and the agreement of that purpose with the independently known character and purposes of the putative agent. Whether, in fact, we have any justification to regard any events as due to divine agency, and whether we can have any independent knowledge of the character and purposes of God, are vexing questions about which theists and atheists argue. The point is, however, that the notion of God as an incorporeal agent cannot be ruled out as unintelligible *a priori,* as Kaplan does.

It is thus logically possible for God to be conceived of as a cosmic agent. And it is also logically necessary, for God to be an adequate object of worship, to be conceived of as having an identifiable character as the "*One* Who is worshiped."[8] For if worship is, as Hartshorne maintains, "the integrating of all one's thoughts and purposes, all valuations and meanings, all perceptions and conceptions,"[9] the God correlative to this integrity of response must be one or individual. Such is the basic Jewish-Christian-Islamic tenet.

Utilizing our criteria, then, I find Kaplan's theological reconstruction lacking in consistency. Kaplan presents a world-picture consisting ultimately of impersonal processes and forces with no integrating agent or cosmic individual unifying these forces in a coherent manner, the only sources of integration being human individuals. I find this world-picture inconsistent with conventional prayer in which God is addressed as Thou, the usage adopted in the Reconstructionist prayer book.

In terms of adequacy, Kaplan's theological work is most valuable for inculcating an awareness of those creative forces and processes in nature and in us that we can identify as manifestations of the divine. But in order to identify these forces as manifestations of the divine, we need a concept of God with more character and specificity than Kaplan's conception of God as the ongoing process of cosmic creativity as generative of human salvation. Without such specificity, a concept of God is not religiously adequate.

Kaplan's pragmatic relevance for Judaism and the Jewish people has been immense. He has given what is perhaps the most concise and yet comprehensive definition of Judaism for modern, liberal Jews—namely, Judaism as the evolving religious civilization of the Jewish people. He has taught and inspired countless rabbis with his intellectual honesty and integrity. Where his pragmatic relevance is most controversial is his theological reconstruction. I believe that Kaplan was right in his rejection of unreflective supernaturalism. But he has thrown out the baby with the bathwater. If God is merely the name we give to the sum total of all the creative forces and relationships in nature and in humans, this reality is too amorphous to be worthy of worship. Moreover, if God is identified solely with the good, how is evil explained? Kaplan attributes evil to the chaos in nature and in humans not yet "invaded by creativity." But here Kaplan fails to reckon with entropy and the second law of thermodynamics, according to which the universe is running down. Kaplan needs a metaphysical concept such as a cosmic ground of creativity to lend support to his thesis that creativity is forever conquering chaos. Furthermore, by identifying God solely with the good, Kaplan threatens the monotheistic structure of Judaism, implying a dualism of God versus negative forces that are beyond God's control.

This is a major problem for the religious naturalist. If God is, as Whitehead maintains, "in the world or nowhere," there are forces over which God has no control. Granted, as Whitehead maintains, that an omnipotent God who foresaw all the evils and imperfections in the universe and yet created it would not be worthy of worship, how does the religious naturalist defend the view that a God limited in power is worthy of worship?

Kaplan does not answer this question adequately, for an answer requires more metaphysical thinking than his pragmatic orientation allowed. We therefore turn to Alfred North Whitehead and process theology, with its full-scale metaphysics, to see how this question and other theological issues are addressed systematically. Hopefully, we will then be in a position to determine if a sufficiently cogent case for God can be argued.

Notes

[1]Mordecai M. Kaplan, *The Meaning of God in Modern Jewish Religion*. The Jewish Reconstructionist Foundation, 1957, p. 76.

[2]See, for example, Kaplan, *The Future of the American Jew*. Reconstructionist Press, 1967, p. 183 ff.

[3]Kaplan, *The Religion of Ethical Nationhood*. The Macmillan Co., 1970, p. 51.

[4]William E. Kaufman, *Contemporary Jewish Philosophies*. University Press of America, 1985, p. 210.

[5]Alfred North Whitehead, *Religion in the Making*. Meridian Books, 1967, p. 148.

[6]Kaplan, *The Future of the American Jew*, p. 182f.

[7]See Basil Mitchell, *The Justification of Religious Belief*. Oxford University Press, 1981, p. 7f.

[8]Charles Hartshorne, *A Natural Theology for Our Time*. Open Court Publishing Co., 1967, p. 3.

[9]*Ibid.*, p. 4f.

5

Creativity and the Cosmic Adventure

The years of study of Mordecai M. Kaplan's religious naturalism led me to explore the process philosophical thought of Alfred North Whitehead. Finding Kaplan's theology suggestive in its notion of God as process, but metaphysically incomplete as a worldview, I found in the process metaphysics of Whitehead a more systematic approach that I hoped would provide more intellectual satisfaction in my quest for a tenable concept of God. Moreover, Whitehead addressed more directly than Kaplan a problem that bothered me, namely, the challenge of scientific materialism.

49

The Challenge of Scientific Materialism

The worldview of scientific materialism, we have seen, with its "picture" of "atoms and the void" as the ultimate reality, poses a major problem for religious belief in our time. According to this world-picture, the universe consists of matter in motion governed by mechanical laws. The human individual is like a machine, subject to biochemical laws. The human mind is merely an epiphenomenon, an accidental by-product of evolution. Concepts such as the soul and God are purely human constructions, devised to soften the confrontation with brute, material reality, a reality that is ultimately nothing more than a random chance collocation of atoms and molecules.

This worldview is maintained not only by scientifically oriented philosophers such as Russell and Quine but is also prominent in literature. The British novelist Somerset Maugham, in his autobiography, explains how this conception of the universe undermined his religious belief:

> I read a great many books. They told me that man was a machine subject to mechanical laws; and when the machine ran down that was the end of him. I saw men die at the hospital and my startled sensibilities confirmed what my books had taught me. I was satisfied to believe that religion and the idea of God were constructions that the human race had evolved as a convenience for living, and represented something that had at one time, and for all I was prepared to say still had, value for the survival of the species, but that must be historically explained, and correspond to nothing real. I called myself an agnostic, but in my blood and bones I looked upon God as an hypothesis that a reasonable man must reject.[1]

We have observed that there are legitimate reasons for a reasonable person to reject the notion of God as a cosmic bookkeeper. But there are other ways to conceive of God. Can any of them meet Maugham's argument? In this chapter, we examine a possible answer to the challenge of Maugham's materialism and an alternative to the traditional religious picture: the new worldview of process theology. Although developed in Chicago and now centered in southern California, the movement is worldwide and includes theologians who are Anglican, Roman Catholic, and Methodist, among other Protestant denominations.

Alfred North Whitehead: Biographical Data

Process theology is based on the philosophy of Alfred North Whitehead. Whitehead's career was a tale of three cities: Cambridge, England; London; and Cambridge, Massachusetts. Born in Ramsgate, Kent, in England in 1861, Whitehead was the son of an Anglican clergyman. Educated at Trinity College, Cambridge, Whitehead became a Fellow of Trinity and taught mathematics there for a quarter of a century. This was followed by thirteen years in the same field at the University of London. In 1924, at the age of sixty-three, Whitehead was invited to become a professor of philosophy at Harvard University. Then began appearing such major works from his pen as *Science and the Modern World* in 1925, *Process and Reality* in 1929, *Adventures of Ideas* in 1933, and *Modes of Thought* in 1938. Whitehead died at Cambridge, Massachusetts, in 1947 at the age of eighty-seven.

A major turning point in Whitehead's thinking occurred in the last decade of the nineteenth century, when he was a student at the University of Cambridge in England. He explains that when he went to Cambridge, everything was supposed to be known about physics that could be known— except for a few things, such as electromagnetic phenomena, which remained to be coordinated with Newtonian physics.[2] But by 1900, the principles of Newtonian physics were demolished. Whitehead describes how this influenced him:

> By 1900 the Newtonian physics were demolished, done for! Speaking personally, it had a profound effect on me; I have been fooled once, and I'll be

damned if I'll be fooled again! Einstein is supposed
to have made an epochal discovery. I am respectful
and interested, but also skeptical. There is no more
reason to suppose that Einstein's relativity is anything final, than Newton's *Principia*.[3]

The moral Whitehead derived was that there is no point
when we can say, "Now, at last, we have certitude." For this
reason, Whitehead developed a new picture to deal with a
universe whose possibilities are infinite. This is the world-
picture of process theology.

A New World-Picture

Can one maintain the theory of evolution and still
believe in God? Religious fundamentalists are threatened
by the theory of evolution. In contrast, Whitehead sees the
spiritual possibilities of an evolutionary outlook, a process
worldview. Describing his point of view, Whitehead says:

I am, as you see, a thorough-going evolutionist.
Millions of years ago our earth began to cool off and
forms of life began in their simplest aspects. Where
did they come from? They must have been inherent
in the total scheme of things; they must have
existed in potentiality in the most minute
particles....It doesn't strike me as at all impossible
that the smallest pebble might contain within it a
universe as complex as the one we know, and that
the universe or universes which we have recently
begun to apprehend may be as minute in the scale
of what lies beyond as that in the pebble to the one
we know; or that the vastness might be much
greater in the opposite direction—the direction of
what we consider the infinitely small.[4]

Already we begin to see the difference in outlook
between Whitehead on the one hand and Russell and
Quine on the other. Russell and Quine seek simplicity and
precision; they seek to shave off excess baggage in
formulating their picture of the world. In contrast, Whitehead

has a sense for the infinite possibilities of the cosmos. Thus he asserts, "Here we are with our finite beings and physical senses in the presence of a universe whose possibilities are infinite, and even though we may not apprehend them, these infinite possibilities are actualities."[5]

Whitehead's world-picture is an expansive one, one that compels us to stretch our imagination, to transcend our finite perspectives. Yet there is an obstacle to our self-transcendence: language. A recurrent theme in Whitehead's philosophy is his emphasis on the inadequacy of language to express our deepest thoughts. He explains: "I am impressed by the inadequacy of language to express our conscious thought, and by the inadequacy of our conscious thought to express our subconscious. The curse of philosophy has been the supposition that language is an exact medium."[6]

Why is language inadequate? Language is limited because it is relative to our notion of size; we tend to measure everything in proportion to our bodies. But from what science has discovered about the infinitely small and the infinitely vast, the size of our bodies is almost totally irrelevant. The heavens with all their vastness, Whitehead says, may be only a minute strand of tissue in the body of a being in the scale of which all universes are as a trifle. We have just begun to understand that such vastness exists. "Only at rare moments," Whitehead writes, "does that deeper and vaster world come through into the conscious thought or expression; these are the memorable moments of our lives, when we feel—when we know—we are being used as instruments of a greater force than ourselves for purposes higher and wider than our own."[7]

Here, then, is a man of science whose world-picture is wide enough to encompass a mystical way of knowing God. Let us explore his world-picture in depth.

Whitehead invites us to look at the world in an entirely new way. His first step is to urge us to give up completely the habit of picturing the material world as composed of enduring elements or substances moving about in an otherwise empty space. He utilizes the insights of contemporary physicists who substitute vibratory entities for Newtonian corpuscles, and electromagnetic and gravitational fields for apparently empty space. The material world, in Whitehead's view, becomes a series of events and processes. Even a mountain, in his view, is a result of a long process: a structure persisting through a connected series of events.

What is the ultimate or basic event for Whitehead? Here we come to another parting of the ways between Russell and Quine on the one hand and Whitehead on the other. Unlike these thinkers, Whitehead sees nature as alive. The basic event, which Whitehead calls an "actual entity" or "actual occasion," is a momentary feeling or experience. How and why did Whitehead arrive at this notion that these actual entities are the ultimate metaphysical units?

Whitehead's target is our usual dualistic picture of human beings and nature. According to this dualistic way of looking at things, which goes back to seventeenth-century philosopher Descartes, reality is split into two poles: inert matter on the one hand, the human mind on the other. With the rise of science in the seventeenth century, we began to regard ourselves as spectators and users of nature. Bacon paved the way for science and technology with his aphorism: "Knowledge is power." Nature became an object apart from us, inanimate and lifeless, which we could use and harness for our purposes. This was a double-edged sword: It increased our knowledge and control but led to our estrangement and alienation from nature. Whitehead calls this the bifurcation of nature, splitting it into the domain of mind, on the one hand, and matter on the other. The bifurcation of nature, giving rise to our sense of alienation, leads directly to the existential feeling dramatized by Sartre and Camus of being a "stranger" in the universe, not an organic part of the whole. Whitehead's philosophy is precisely an effort to restore a sense of wholeness to human existence, to see humans and our experience as part of nature and to see nature as generative of experience.

It is Whitehead's speculative hypothesis that human experience is the clue to the ultimate nature of things. In the twentieth century, the physical sciences have become open to the possibility that the notion of matter does not illuminate what they investigate. So long as atoms were regarded as the ultimate stuff of the universe, the notion of matter as little lumps of impenetrable stuff, having definite location and moving continuously through space, seemed appropriate. Mechanical models could be employed to understand them.

But when the atom was discovered not to be ultimate but rather to be composed of electrons, protons, and empty space, problems arose. These entities functioned both as particles of matter and as waves. A similar duality in the functioning of light had long puzzled investigators. It thus seemed that the ultimate entities composing the world functioned sometimes as particles, sometimes as waves. Moreover, these entities seemed to be able to move from place to place without passing through the intervening space. Furthermore, it became clear that protons and electrons are not material things that carry electric charges but rather are electric charges. Something happens, now here, then there, with definite connections between one event and the next, but without continuous movement between them. Things happen in bursts or jerks rather than in an even flow.

Whitehead's idea is to think of these electronic events as occasions of electronic experience. Experience here does not imply sense experience, consciousness, or imagination. Rather, what Whitehead is hypothesizing is that these electronic events, which he called occasions of experience, are discrete and indivisible units of feeling, succeeding each other with a rapidity beyond any grasp of conscious attention—the direct analysis of a single occasion of experience being impossible.[8]

Whitehead is suggesting, then, that the entities in nature are to be thought of as belonging to the same category of existence as human experience. His working hypothesis is that the structure of every organism is analogous to that of an occasion of experience, or, more broadly, that the structure of every electronic event in nature is analogous to the structure of an occasion of human experience. Thus Whitehead is striving to develop a system in which there is coherence of all human experience and all of nature. I will present a more inclusive account of his system in the next section, where I introduce his new understanding of God.

In any event, it should now be clear what Whitehead would say of the atoms and the void world-picture of Quine, and of British empirical thinkers and writers such as Russell and Maugham. Whitehead's thesis is that the materialist worldview is built on a mistaken conception, which he calls the fallacy of misplaced concreteness. Whitehead maintains that atoms, molecules, and electrons are abstractions and that the ultimate concrete realities are events or actual occasions that are incipiently mental because they transcend in some measure the causal influence of their past. It is this transcendence that in higher organisms becomes life and intelligence.

The key word here is *process*. *Process* means an ongoing series of events that leads to novelty. Whitehead's picture of the universe is that of a creative movement to novelty—a passage, a constant dynamic flow of events. A flower, a tree, a brook, a pond: All of these are new manifestations of nature, ever evolving, ever renewing itself.

But nature is not only novelty. If it were, there would be nothing but chaos. Nature is also order, structure, harmony. What, then, is the source of nature's order and novelty? How do order and novelty coexist? To account for their existence, Whitehead introduces God into his system.

Whitehead has defined "Speculative Philosophy" as "the endeavor to frame a coherent, logical, necessary system of general ideas in terms of which every element of our experience can be interpreted."[9] He further defines coherence as meaning that "the fundamental ideas, in terms of which the scheme is developed, presuppose each other so that in isolation they are meaningless."[10] Thus, no entity can be conceived in complete abstraction from the universe.

As we explore Whitehead's idea of God, I propose that we investigate two key concerns: first, how his system necessitates a particular idea of God for its coherence; and second, the coherence of the system itself. Clearly the case for Whitehead's God is intrinsically interwoven with the coherence of Whitehead's entire world-picture. We need to determine whether Whitehead's organic worldview, based on human experience as the model, shows itself to be a world hypothesis that has greater explanatory power than our usual dualistic world-picture, which Whitehead refers to pejoratively as the bifurcation of nature. My major concern is to see what light Whitehead sheds on the idea of God, and whether, in fact, he is more successful than previous thinkers in moving us toward God as a reality and not merely as an idea. The success of this venture, as I have been at pains to point out, is tied up with the coherence of his world-picture.

Whitehead's New Idea of God

Whitehead identifies God as a factor in human experience, immanent in the world. Accordingly, unlike most other philosophies of religion, Whitehead's does not focus on proof for the existence of God, for the aim of such proofs is to provide rational grounds for the existence of a transcendent being, a creator of the universe. The existence of such a deity is to be inferred from aspects of the universe rather than being present in our experience. Whitehead rejects this idea of God, not only because it renders God responsible for evil, but for the more fundamental reason that we can know nothing humanly important about God. We know, according to this idea, that "He is such a being as to design and create the universe, and there our knowledge stops."[11]

It is, rather, Whitehead's thesis that we cannot rise above the actual world and know anything beyond it. We can only discover the factors disclosed in the world as experienced. Thus, we may discover an immanent God, but not a God wholly transcendent.

The burden of Whitehead's thesis, then, is that God is a factor in human experience and a formative metaphysical element in the world. In *Religion in the Making*,[12] Whitehead identifies the formative elements in the world as follows:

1) The creativity whereby the actual world has the character of temporal passage to novelty.
2) The realm of ideal entities, or forms, not actual but exemplified in everything actual.
3) The actual but nontemporal entity whereby the indeterminacy of mere creativity is transmuted into a determinate freedom. This nontemporal entity is what persons call God—the supreme God of rational religion.

A key question is, Why is it necessary to introduce God as a factor in the world? For Whitehead, the necessity lies in the following considerations. Whitehead sees the world as a vast network of momentary events or actual entities coming into being and then lapsing into the past. Each new event, to be an event, must take account of other events that make up its world and must do so in a definite way, for without definiteness there is no actuality. Now, if the form of definiteness derived only from the past, the actual entity would exhibit no freedom or spontaneity. Thus, the form of definiteness must be derived from the realm of possibility. But the realm of possibility is purely abstract; it lacks agency. "There must be an agency that mediates between these abstract forms or pure possibilities and the actual world."[13] This factor, for Whitehead, is God, who envisages the eternal objects, the abstract forms of definiteness, in such a way as to establish their graded relevance to each new situation in the world. God is "that factor in the universe which establishes what is not as relevant to what is, and lures the world toward new forms of realization."[14]

To illustrate, let us consider an occasion of experience. Each occasion of experience is influenced by its past, the state of one's body, and conditions in the wider world out of which the event arises. Whitehead calls this aspect of human experience the mode of causal efficacy. But it is

Whitehead's contention that the efficacy of the past is not a complete explanation of the event. He holds that every event transcends its past; freedom and self-determination are involved in every occasion of experience. How is it possible that in this moment a decision can be made that was not determined by its past?

Every occasion has a subjective aim shaped by things independent of our will. The initial phase of the subjective aim is God's immanence in each occasion. God is present in the call to possibility, the lure of feeling toward unrealized ideals beyond what the past compels us to become. An example from literature nicely illustrates Whitehead's point. In his novel *Of Time and the River*, Thomas Wolfe describes his protagonist Eugene Gant, standing on the platform of the train station in the North Carolina town of his birth, waiting for the train to take him to the North. Wolfe describes "the ecstatic tension of that train's approach," an occasion of experience in which "he could feel, taste, smell and see everything with an instant still intensity."[15] In that instant the lure of possibility opens up, "for he had dreamed and hungered for the proud unknown North with that wild ecstasy, that intolerable and wordless joy of longing and desire, which only a Southerner can feel."[16] This description of the not-yet impinging on the now, the telic or purposive dimension in human experience, the lure of novelty, the freedom of self-transcendence, the attainment of value—these are the elements in immediate experience that Whitehead identifies as God's gift to us.

But why identify these aspects of human experience as manifestations of the divine? What is the justification for Whitehead's redefinition of God? The reason lies in the following considerations. The word *God* is heavily laden with oppressive, negative, and superstitious overtones. When people experience illness, tragedy, the death of loved ones, they often ask, "Why did God do this to me?" They may become angry at God, conceived of as a punishing, vindictive agent, and lose faith. This is one of the roots of atheism. Clearly, we can understand why Whitehead is trying to develop an alternative conception of God.

A character in Tennessee Williams' play *Suddenly Last Summer* says that we are all children in a vast kindergarten, trying to spell the name of God with the wrong alphabet blocks. According to Whitehead, what has been wrong with the theologies of the historical Western religions is the fact that they have been trying to spell the name of God with the wrong idea-blocks. Whitehead explains:

> The notion of God as the "unmoved mover" is derived from Aristotle, at least so far as Western thought is conceived. The notion of God as "eminently real" is a favourite doctrine of Christian theology. The combination of the two into the doctrine of an aboriginal, eminently real, transcendent creator, at whose fiat the world came into being, and whose imposed will it obeys, is the fallacy which has infused tragedy into the histories of Christianity and Mahometanism.

> When the Western world accepted Christianity, Caesar conquered....The Church gave unto God the attributes which belonged exclusively to Caesar.[17]

That kind of theology fitted into a despotically oriented world, contributing to evil even then. But, Whitehead contends, this idea is inappropriate for a democratically oriented society.

Accordingly, instead of associating God with tyranny, destruction, and death, Whitehead is suggesting new building blocks for the edifice of theology: The words he uses to identify the divine are value, freedom, novelty, spontaneity, and possibility. The word *God* is referent to those factors in the universe that are worthy of our trust. "The purpose of God," writes Whitehead, "is the attainment of value in the temporal world."[18] On this view, God lures us to the realization of value in every moment and urges us to constitute the moment so that it will contribute value to the future. To summarize: Whitehead maintains that the cosmic activity through which relevant potentiality becomes effective in each occasion of experience is properly called "God." More precisely, this is the *primordial* nature of God—God as the organ of novelty. As John B. Cobb, Jr., expresses it, "No event occurs in the world without God's coming, not as a part of the past, determining world, but as the gift of freedom, the gift of transcendence, the gift of the future."[19]

But how does the process thinker deal with those negative aspects of experience—failure, loss, tragedy, destruction, and death—which are precisely those elements that drive people to atheism? To address these is partly the function of Whitehead's concept of the *consequent* nature of God. By "consequent," Whitehead means that God's "prehension" or taking account of the past is consequent upon the way the world constitutes itself. "The consequent nature of God," writes Whitehead, "is his judgment on the world. He saves the world as it passes into the immediacy of his own life. It is the judgment of a tenderness which loses nothing that can be saved. It is also the judgment of a wisdom which uses what in the temporal process is mere wreckage."[20] God thus immortalizes the past by incorporating it into God's own everlasting life. And God transmutes evil into an eternal harmony:

> God has in his nature the knowledge of evil, of pain and degradation, but it is there overcome with what is good. Every fact is what it is, a fact of pleasure, of joy, of pain or of suffering. In its union with God that fact is not a total loss, but on its finer side is an element to be woven immortally into the rhythm of mortal things. Its very evil becomes a stepping stone in all embracing ideal of God.[21]

The implication here is that God grows and is affected by the world. That is what is meant by *process theology*: The consequent nature of God is in process. But God is also more than process, for God is everlasting. As everlasting, God is the source of permanence amid the flux of perpetual perishing, immortalizing the past by incorporating it into

God's memory, transmuting it into God's ideal harmony. Whitehead's process theology represents a new approach to the problem of evil. God does not unilaterally intervene to prevent evil, but God and the creatures jointly can transmute evil into good, a goodness woven into God's ideal harmony.

Thus, God does not do the weaving alone. We cannot do what we please and simply rely upon God to transmute the evil and wreckage of our lives into God's ideal harmony. Quite to the contrary, Whitehead emphatically asserts, "It is as true to say that God creates the World, as that the World creates God."[22] What Whitehead is asserting is that we play a role in shaping and participating in the everlasting divine life. We and God together, on this view, are co-creators of the future: What we do becomes part of the divine life. Whitehead here lends richness and depth to the ancient Judaic rabbinic conception of humans and God as partners in creation; what he adds is the notion that what we do is actually incorporated into the divine life and memory. But it is also clear that Whitehead's new idea of God diverges markedly from the traditional Judeo-Christian concept of the deity.

The traditional notion of God is that of a transcendent omnipotent being who created the universe. Whitehead vehemently opposes this concept. He asserts that "it was a mistake, as the Hebrews tried, to conceive of God as creating the world from outside, at one go. An all-foreseeing Creator, who could have made this world as we find it now—what could we think of such a being? Foreseeing everything and yet putting into it all sorts of imperfections...outrageous ideas."[23]

Against this traditional notion, Whitehead puts the accent on the immanence of God:

> God is in the world or nowhere, creating continually in and around us. The creative principle is everywhere, in inanimate nature and so-called inanimate matter, in the ether, water, earth, human hearts. But this creation is a continuing process, and the

process is itself the actuality, since no sooner do you arrive than you start on a fresh journey. Insofar as man partakes of this creative process does he partake of the divine, of God, and that participation is his immortality, reducing the question of whether his individuality survives death of the body to the state of an irrelevancy. His true destiny as co-creator in the universe is his dignity and his grandeur.[24]

The first thing to notice about Whitehead's God is that this deity is not omnipotent. God as the "tendency in the universe to produce worthwhile things," Whitehead admits, "is by no means omnipotent. Other forces work against it."[25]

Second, Whitehead associates the notion of a transcendent God with the Hebrews and credits the Greeks with the idea of "creation as going on everywhere all the time within the universe."[26] He fails to recognize that the Hebrews conceived of God both as transcendent and immanent. God, according to the Hebrew Daily Prayer Book, renews his creation every day. Creation as a continuous process is as much a Hebraic as a Greek idea.

Third, Whitehead proposes a finite or limited God because of the evil and imperfection in the world. "The limitation of God," Whitehead has written, "is his goodness."[27]

What, then, does God do? How does God act? Whitehead's God works by persuasion rather than force. "He is the lure for feeling, the eternal urge of desire....he is the poet of the world, with tender patience leading it by his vision of truth, beauty, and goodness."[28] God thus does not impose order on the world but is rather the source of possible patterns, luring the cosmos at each stage of its process toward the actualization of new possibilities. There is indeterminacy in nature and in us; the universe of process theology is open and not rigid. It may be said that in Whitehead's system, God proposes, but the event disposes. Whitehead's God offers possibilities and potentialities but no guarantees. To be sure, God maintains a

64 The Case for God

sufficient ratio of order and novelty to sustain the universe in adequate fashion. But whether God's ideals are realized depends on God's creatures. Both nature and human beings possess autonomy; otherwise, there would be no novelty in the world.

There is another aspect of Whitehead's God that is significant. This is the aesthetic component whereby God evokes intensity of feeling: "God's purpose in the creative advance is the evocation of intensities."[29] One interpreter of Whitehead refers to this aspect of God's activity as the cosmic adventure. By "adventure" is meant "the universe's search for continually more intense forms of ordered novelty."[30] If we consider the hierarchy of being, we see an advance in complexity throughout evolution. The intensity of the synthesis of order and novelty, progressing from the animal cell to the animal brain and then to the human brain, gives us a hint of the adventurous experimentation with fresh forms that exists in our cosmos.

The world-picture that emerges from Whitehead's philosophy, then, is that of a universe constantly in process, lured by a God who "inspires" ongoing adventure, novelty, and creativity, and who, at the same time, provides sufficient order and permanence for the world process to be sustained. Whitehead refers to God as "the great companion—the fellow-sufferer who understands."[31] What his vision of God offers is the sense of being encompassed by a universal trustworthy process infinitely larger and more important than ourselves and the feeling that we are not alone in life's struggle, because God suffers as we suffer. God, according to this picture, cannot "save" us from illness, tragedy, or death. God does not intervene to redeem the oppressed, so we cannot blame God for the Holocaust or other human ills. But God does "save" us in the sense of preserving a memory of us in God's eternal vision. Through his concept of God, Whitehead invests the passage of time with pathos, for amid the perpetual perishing of finite creatures, there is a cosmic companion who understands, remembers, and cherishes our highest values.

Evaluation of Whitehead's God-Idea
From a Religious Standpoint

We are now in a position to evaluate Whitehead's idea of God and his world-picture. First, let us examine his idea of God *internally*, that is, from the standpoint of its religious availability. We seek to determine whether Whitehead's God is truly worthy of worship. Then, in the following section, we shall evaluate his world-picture and God-idea externally, based on our criteria of consistency, adequacy to the facts of experience, and pragmatic value.

My evaluation of Whitehead's God from a religious standpoint is necessarily based on the Judaic tradition, the foundation of my own religious thinking. On the one hand, Whitehead's idea of God is noteworthy because it alleviates the oppressive burden of striving to reconcile the alleged omnipotence of God with God's failure to intervene to save six million Jews from Hitler's Holocaust. Whitehead is an important resource because according to his philosophical thought, God's activity in the universe is simply not in accord with the traditional categories: God is not a supernatural deity who intervenes to rescue us from evil. Rather, Whitehead's deity envisages possibilities, establishing their graded relevance to each new situation. God's purpose is the attainment of value in the temporal world, and the conserving of value in God's consequent nature. Since Whitehead's God does not "operate" in the same way as the biblical God, it makes no sense to ask about Whitehead's God, as is frequently asked about the biblical God, "Why did God not intervene to prevent the Holocaust?"

This is surely an advantage in Whitehead's philosophy. But now a question arises concerning the religious legitimacy of Whitehead's reinterpretation of the God-idea, namely, whether there is sufficient continuity between Whitehead's idea of God and the traditional notion to warrant the use of the name *God* for Whitehead's deity.

On the face of it, there seems to be an overwhelming gap between the traditional idea and Whitehead's notion. "The basic idea of Israelite religion," writes the biblical scholar Yehezkel Kaufmann, "is that God is supreme over all. There is no realm above or beside him to limit his absolute sovereignty. He is utterly distinct from, and other than, the world; he is subject to no laws, no compulsions, or powers that transcend him."[32] Yet this same writer recognizes the problems of the concept, as in various biblical passages in which God is said to cause humans to sin. He explains:

> While it is axiomatic that sin is man's doing, the religious consciousness of the Bible was unable to reconcile itself entirely with this restriction of God's dominion. *There is a tension here between the moral demand that sets limits to the working of God and the religious demand that subjects all to divine control.*[33]

Kaufmann admits that one can discern

> ...a primary non-moral or supra-moral element in monotheistic faiths: the will and command of God is absolutely good. The doctrine of predestination held by some Christian denominations is the most striking form of this idea. God has foreordained who will be saved and who will be damned. At this point the absolute will of God becomes in essence immoral; monotheism approaches paganism.[34]

It was precisely against this identification of the will of God as absolutely good, even if it amounts to foreordaining who will be saved and who will be damned, that John Stuart Mill inveighed in this famous passage:

> Whatever power such a being may have over me, there is one thing which he shall not do; he shall not compel me to worship him. I will call no being good who is not what I mean when I apply that epithet to my fellow creatures; and if such a being can sentence me to hell for not so calling him, to hell I will go.[35]

Surely, therefore, because of the tension of the moral and religious demands inherent in the traditional notion of

God, Whitehead is morally justified in asserting that the limitation of God is God's goodness. Yet Whitehead is at such pains to demolish the idea of God as an imperial ruler that he goes to the opposite extreme and negates God's ultimacy. The crucial passage is the following:

> Neither God, nor the World, reaches static completion. Both are in the grip of the ultimate metaphysical ground, the creative advance into novelty. Either of them, God and the World, is the instrument of novelty for the other.[36]

Why does Whitehead take this drastic step? Dr. John B. Cobb, Jr., a leading interpreter of Whitehead and the director of the Center for Process Studies in Claremont, California, admits that from the perspective of traditional Western theism, the identification of God with anything less that the ultimate appears paradoxical.[37] He attributes Whitehead's radical move precisely to his conviction that the object of authentic religious concern must be characterized more decisively by goodness than by metaphysical ultimacy.[38] Here Whitehead stands in the tradition of John Stuart Mill.

Nevertheless, Cobb is not satisfied with the apparent subordination of God's creative role to creativity and therefore argues for the need, within the context of Whitehead's own presuppositions, for a greater creative role to be attributed to God.

Cobb compares the role of creativity in Whitehead's philosophy to the role of prime matter in Aristotle's thought.[39] If one asks of Aristotelian philosophy the question why it is that there is anything at all, the answer is that prime matter is eternal and demands some form. But, Cobb maintains, creativity cannot play that role in Whitehead's philosophy. Cobb explains:

> Whitehead, of course, was convinced that the process is everlasting. Creativity will always take new forms, but it will always continue to be unchangingly creative. My point is only that the notion of creativ-

ity in itself provides no grounds for this faith. Hence, as an answer to the question of why there is and continues to be anything at all, creativity cannot play in Whitehead's philosophy quite the role prime matter plays in Aristotle.[40]

Why is this so? In Whitehead's philosophy, every actual occasion is a novel addition to the universe, not only a new form of the same eternal stuff as in Aristotle. Although creativity is an aspect of every such entity, creativity cannot be the answer to the question of why that or any entity occurs. For if occasions ceased to occur, there would be no creativity: Creativity can explain only *ex post facto*. Therefore, Cobb reasons, if the question as to why things are at all is raised in the Whiteheadian context, the answer must lie in the decisions of actual entities. Now the decisive element in the initiation of each actual occasion is the granting to that occasion of an initial aim. The conclusion of Cobb's argument is that since Whitehead attributes this function to God, God must also be conceived of as being the reason that entities occur at all as well as determining the limits within which they achieve their own forms. God's role in creation, within the Whiteheadian scheme itself, is thus more fundamental than Whitehead's own language suggests.[41] Nevertheless, despite his intent to attribute a greater role to God in the context of Whiteheadian philosophy, Cobb insists that he is not claiming either eminent reality or necessary existence for God, but only everlasting existence. Rather, Cobb is arguing, within the Whiteheadian context, that God is the reason that each new occasion arises, but God, past occasions, and the new occasion jointly constitute the reason for what it becomes.[42]

The conclusion of this section is that the tension engendered by the traditional God-idea itself—that is, the tension between the moral and religious demands—gives rise to the reactions of morally sensitive philosophers such as John Stuart Mill and Alfred North Whitehead, with their emphasis on the goodness of God and their willingness to limit God's power. In this sense, these reactions flow from the traditional notion and are continuous with it because they operate within that framework.

More problematic is Whitehead's insistence on denying eminent reality to God. If God is one reality among others, but not the supreme reality, is God worthy of worship? Surely, Whitehead is correct in his assertion that an omnipotent, tyrannical, Oriental-despot type of deity is not worthy of worship. But has he not gone too far in the opposite direction, in denying eminent reality to God? Cobb realizes this problem inherent in Whitehead's radical limitation of God, and attempts to provide a greater role for God as creator. This fact itself indicates the sensitivity of this leading process theologian to Whitehead's radical limitation of God. He is striving to reinterpret Whitehead's philosophy as being more in consonance with traditional notions than it appears to be on the surface.

Another prominent process philosopher and interpreter of Whitehead, Charles Hartshorne, strives to restore God's eminent reality and necessary existence within a Whiteheadian context. Whether his program is successful will be discussed and evaluated in the following chapter.

To summarize: The moral imperative to limit God's absolute control for the sake of maintaining God's goodness flows from the tension within the traditional concept itself. The problem then arises of the ontological status of God within the Whiteheadian context. Whitehead's system itself seems to require a greater role for God than Whitehead is willing to acknowledge. So a tension remains, albeit at a different level, within the system itself. Perhaps there is an inherent tension in the idea of God, and in the conception of God's relation to the world, that impels us to recognize the dialectical character of theology: that whatever we say about God, we are bound to correct by saying something of an opposite character.

Philosophical Evaluation of Whitehead's World-Picture and God-Idea

What elements does Whitehead's philosophical theology add to the case for God? If Whitehead's reflections on God throughout his writings are construed as an argument for the existence of God, it is essentially the traditional argument from the order of the universe to the ground of order. But Whitehead adds a new note to the argument.

The traditional teleological argument, or argument from order or design, was based in Paley's famous version on the analogy of the universe to a machine, such as a watch. Just as the watch implies a watchmaker, so the universe implies a cosmic designer. But this form of the argument was vulnerable to the new understanding of the evolutionary processes in nature, which arose in the nineteenth century. Random variation and survival of the fittest appeared to explain the emergence of new forms in ways that removed the need for an intelligent creator. Nevertheless, problems remained. Although random variation may illumine the emergence of the living from the inorganic, this process has nothing to do with survival of the fittest, for a stone is more capable of survival than a plant or animal. Besides random variation and survival of the fittest, another force seems to be at work in nature: a thrust toward more complex forms of order. The universe appears to be too complex to be random. Furthermore, it seems incredible that from the purely material, inert, passive lumps of matter of the mechanistic theory, life and mind could have emerged.

If the world is viewed as a complex machine, the idea of God that theists infer is that of a creator who stands outside of creation, as the watchmaker transcends the watch. Hume devastatingly criticized this analogy, but Cobb argues:

> If the world is viewed in organic terms, then the principles of life, order and growth must be immanent to the organisms. That there *is* something which we may properly call God is sufficiently indicated by the kind of order that is visible to all. But what that "something" is, where it is, how it functions, these questions can be reflectively con-

sidered only in the light of the categories in terms of which the world is understood.[43]

If we are to construe the theological references in Whitehead's writings as an argument, it is an argument for an immanent deity—more precisely, that nontemporal actual entity that is the source and ground of order. And whether the argument is cogent depends on the adequacy of the description of the world from which the argument begins. So our task is to evaluate Whitehead's description of the world—his world-picture—in order to determine the cogency of the resultant idea of God.

Let us first evaluate Whitehead's world-picture from the standpoint of inner consistency or coherence. Whitehead explicitly states that "God is not to be treated as an exception to all metaphysical principles, invoked to save their collapse. He is their chief exemplification."[44] In other words, God must be conceived in terms of the generic metaphysical principles applying to all actual entities. Now, according to Whitehead's principle of process, the being of an actual entity is constituted by its becoming. Yet Whitehead refers to God as "the actual but *nontemporal* entity whereby the indetermination of mere creativity is transmuted into a determinate freedom."[45] There appears to be a grave inconsistency here, so much so that one critic asserts:

> Nothing is more puzzling about Whitehead than his describing the Primordial Nature as an entity after he has carefully constructed a monumental metaphysics in which all actual entities are considered becomings. He tries to avoid this glaring inconsistency by calling it a nontemporal entity but this only aggravates the problem because, in his metaphysics, all entities are to be understood in terms of process, and process necessarily involves time.[46]

Cobb strives to resolve this problem in his analysis of the relationship of Whitehead's God to time. For Whitehead, time is physical time, and is a perpetual perishing. Actual entities other than God are temporal: As they become, they perish. The primordial nature of God is eternal: It is wholly unaffected by time or process. The consequent nature of God is everlasting: It involves a creative advance, just like time, but the earlier elements are not lost as new ones are added. To reconcile the apparent contradiction of the two natures of God, Cobb interprets Whitehead to be saying "that God as a whole is everlasting, but that he envisages all possibility eternally."[47] Thus, it is held, there is no contradiction here but rather God is to be conceived as dipolar: eternal in the primordial nature, envisaging all the possibilities; everlasting and therefore temporal in the consequent nature, which implies that there is process in God.

Aware of the difficulty of conceiving of God as an actual entity and yet attributing to God both nontemporal and temporal characteristics, Cobb maintains that it makes more sense within the Whiteheadian context itself to regard God as a living person rather than as an actual entity. A living person is a succession of moments of experience with special continuity. God at any moment would be an actual entity, but viewed retrospectively and prospectively God would be an infinite succession of divine occasions of experience. Because Whitehead attributes to God basic efficacy in the provision of the initial aim for each occasion, God's causal efficacy for the world is like the efficacy of completed occasions for subsequent occasions and not like that of the phases of the becoming of a single occasion for its successors. Because of this and other considerations, Cobb maintains that it is more consistent with Whitehead's own system to think of God as a living person rather than an actual entity.

It is clear why Cobb must make this move in an attempt to save Whitehead's system from inconsistency. The fundamental principle of Whitehead's metaphysics is that ultimate reality resides in actual entities. Whitehead states:

> "Actual entities"—also termed "actual occasions"—
> are the final real things of which the world is made
> up. There is no going beyond actual entities to find

anything more real. They differ among themselves: God is an actual entity, and so is the most trivial puff of existence in far-off empty space. But, though there are gradations of importance, and diversities of function, yet in the principles which actuality exemplifies all are on the same level. The final facts are, all alike, actual entities; and these actual entities are drops of experience, complex and inter-dependent.[48]

Clearly, Whitehead means to say that God is more than "a drop of experience." At the very least, Whitehead means to say that God is a unique actual entity, the principle of concretion necessary for the existence of ordinary actual entities, for these cannot exist without definiteness. In this sense, God may be conceived of as the creator of each actual entity, but of course this decidedly does not mean that God created the world *ex nihilo*. Hence, within the Whiteheadian context, whether God is conceived of as a unique actual entity or as a living person, God is not on the same ontological level as ordinary actual entities, and thus there remains an element of inconsistency and incoherence in Whitehead's metaphysics.

But overall coherence is achieved in the sense that God and the other elements in Whitehead's system do require each other. The specific element of incoherence arises from Whitehead's insistence that God and other actual entities are on the same ontological level, whereas his system actually requires a greater role for God.

Whitehead's idea is that of a dipolar God: God as primordial, eternal in the envisagement of possibilities, yet everlasting and temporal in God's consequent nature, in process with the world. He explains:

The nature of God is dipolar. He has a primordial and a consequent nature. The consequent nature of God is conscious; and it is the realization of the actual world in the unity of his nature, and through the transformation of his wisdom. The primordial nature is conceptual, the consequent nature is the weaving of God's physical feelings upon his primordial concepts.[49]

One difficulty here is how the primordial nature can be both free and also "actually deficient, and unconscious,"[50] as it envisages all the possibilities eternally. The other difficulty is: Given the two natures of God, what is the principle of their unity? Perhaps it is a dialectical unity, a unity of opposites. To be sure, the idea of God as infinite in some respects and finite in other, different respects opens up new vistas for theological thought—namely, the notion of a God of adventure, of inner complexity, who lures the cosmic process toward greater complexity and further intensification of beauty. But the nature of the "inner dialectic" of this dipolar God needs further exploration.

In terms of adequacy to the facts of human experience, Whitehead's world-picture is exciting and relevant if we accept his initial premise that there must be a single type of reality explanatory of both mind and matter, and that the model for understanding ultimate reality must arise from human experience. The problem here is that not everyone is willing to accept human experience as the basic root metaphor. For example, Stephen Pepper in *World Hypotheses* writes concerning this metaphor:

> This view of the world is the only one in which a man feels completely at home. It is perhaps as well for us to learn early, therefore, that we shall probably never feel completely at home in a world view that is adequate. For the world does not seem to be made after man's own image.[51]

In other words, we often experience the world as recalcitrant to our wishes, hopes, and aspirations. Has Whitehead taken sufficient account of our experience of the harshness and opacity of the world to our efforts to feel at home in it? Whitehead's notion of the consequent nature of God is his response to the "wreckage" of the world. And his use of experience as the root metaphor can be defended by asking: Where else can we turn for the ultimate metaphor?

Finally, the pragmatic value of Whitehead's world-picture is its very complexity and richness. His world-picture of creativity and the cosmic adventure, lured by a God both eternal in some aspects, in process in other respects, fosters a striving in us for deeper levels of cognitive and aesthetic experience in response to God's lure.

What elements, then does Whitehead's world-picture add to the case for God? The study of Whitehead's philosophical theology adds new depth and vitality to the teleological argument for the existence of God. Here is a philosopher, mathematician, and man of science, thoroughly conversant with the theory of evolution, whose system opens us up to the possibility that the world is too complex to be random. He awakens us to the possibility of a principle of order immanent in the cosmic process, a formative factor explanatory of the definiteness within nature that cannot be explained simply by random variations. Moreover, as the notion of God becomes more developed in his writings, it becomes clear that God is not only a principle or factor in the universe but an individual who has character, "the poet of the world, with tender patience leading it by his vision of truth, beauty, and goodness"[52]—in short, a God with whom one can enter into a relationship of communion and trust. This is the aspect of Whitehead's God that I find most significant.

The naturalism of Mordecai M. Kaplan engenders in one the feeling that to attribute any kind of sentience to God is a misleading anthropomorphism. Whitehead's emphasis on a connected universe of feeling, and on a God in process who responds to this universe, generates the possibility that one can be scientifically oriented and still retain the notion of a God that is in some sense personal. For Whitehead, to assert that God is only an idea is to set up a false abstraction. As an actual entity, God makes a difference in actual events. Whether Whitehead's God can be interpreted as a living person, as Cobb maintains, is a question for further Whiteheadian scholarship.

Charles Hartshorne, a Whiteheadian process philosopher, but also a major thinker in his own right, has remarked that every philosophical system has an impasse somewhere. To be sure, there are inconsistencies and impasses in Whitehead's metaphysical system. But its richness and its insights disclose new avenues to take in exploring the case for God. In particular, Whitehead's idea of the dipolar God is rich in its suggestiveness.

What we learn from it is that there is a dialectic built into the very idea of God: Whatever we say about God, we are bound to be correct by its polar opposite. In the following chapter, we examine how Charles Hartshorne develops this idea of the dipolar God with greater philosophical rigor. We are accustomed to thinking of God as monopolar: as absolute, transcendent, independent of the existence of the universe. The notion of a dipolar God is that of a deity absolute in some respects, relative in others. It is the exact antithesis of the Thomistic notion of God as Pure Act, as an absolutely simple being. Intuitively, we realize that, if God exists, God far exceeds us in the divine inner complexity. A complex world requires a complex God. But how can the divine complexity, and the dialectical unity of this complexity, be envisaged? And who could possibly claim knowledge of it? Charles Hartshorne is, incredibly, a man who would know God. His is the ideal philosophy to be utilized to sum up and crystallize the case for God and the responses to the nonbeliever. An examination of his thought will cast in bold relief the strengths and weaknesses of theistic belief.

Notes

[1]W. Somerset Maugham, *The Summing Up*. Mentor Books, 1946, p. 155f.
[2]*Dialogues of Alfred North Whitehead* as recorded by Lucien Price. Little, Brown and Co., 1954, p. 345.
[3]*Ibid.*
[4]*Ibid.*, p. 346.
[5]*Ibid.*, p. 134.
[6]*Ibid.*, p. 368.
[7]*Ibid.*, p. 369.
[8]For the foregoing discussion of actual occasions, I have relied on John B. Cobb, Jr., *A Christian Natural Theology: Based on the Thought*

of Alfred North Whitehead. The Westminster Press, 1965, pp. 28–40.
⁹Alfred North Whitehead, *Process and Reality,* Corrected Edition edited by David Ray Griffin and Donald W. Sherburne. The Free Press, 1978, p. 3.
¹⁰*Ibid.*
¹¹Whitehead, *Religion in the Making.* World Publishing Co., 1960, p. 68.
¹²*Ibid.*, p. 88.
¹³John B. Cobb, Jr., and David Ray Griffin, *Process Theology: An Introductory Exposition.* The Westminster Press, 1976, p. 43.
¹⁴*Ibid.*
¹⁵Thomas Wolfe, *Of Time and the River.* Charles Scribner's Sons, 1935, p. 22f.
¹⁶*Ibid.*, p. 23f.
¹⁷Whitehead, *Process and Reality,* p. 342.
¹⁸Whitehead, *Religion in the Making,* p. 97.
¹⁹John B. Cobb, Jr., *Process Theology as Political Theology.* The Westminster Press, 1982, p. 75.
²⁰Whitehead, *Process and Reality,* p. 346.
²¹Whitehead, *Religion in the Making,* p. 149.
²²Whitehead, *Process and Reality,* p. 348.
²³*Dialogues of Alfred North Whitehead,* p. 370.
²⁴*Ibid.*, p. 370f.
²⁵*Ibid.*, p. 370.
²⁶*Ibid.*
²⁷Whitehead, *Religion in the Making,* p. 147.
²⁸Whitehead, *Process and Reality,* pp. 344, 346.
²⁹*Ibid.*, p. 105.
³⁰John F. Haught, *The Cosmic Adventure.* The Paulist Press, 1984, p. 130.
³¹Whitehead, *Process and Reality,* p. 351.
³²Yehezkel Kaufmann, *The Religion of Israel,* tr. and abridged by Moshe Greenberg. University of Chicago Press, 1960, p. 60.
³³*Ibid.*, p. 75; italics added.
³⁴*Ibid.*
³⁵John Stuart Mill, selection from *An Examination of Sir William Hamilton's Philosophy* included as an appendix in *Theism,* edited by Richard Taylor. The Liberal Arts Press, 1957, pp. 89–96.
³⁶Whitehead, *Process and Reality,* p. 349.
³⁷Cobb, *A Christian Natural Theology,* p. 143.
³⁸*Ibid.*
³⁹*Ibid.*, p. 206ff.
⁴⁰*Ibid.*, p. 211.
⁴¹*Ibid.*, p. 211f.
⁴²*Ibid.*, p. 214.
⁴³*Ibid.*, p. 173.
⁴⁴Whitehead, *Process and Reality,* p. 343.

[45]Whitehead, *Religion in the Making*, p. 88; italics added.

[46]Edward H. Madden and Peter H. Hare, *Evil and the Concept of God*. Charles C. Thomas, Publisher, 1968, p. 118f.

[47]Cobb, *A Christian Natural Theology*, p. 87.

[48]Whitehead, *Process and Reality*, p. 18.

[49]*Ibid.*, p. 345.

[50]*Ibid.*

[51]Stephen C. Pepper, *World Hypotheses*. University of California Press, 1970, p. 120.

[52]Whitehead, *Process and Reality*, p. 346.

6

In
Defense
of
God

During my stay in San Antonio, Texas, I enjoyed an intellectual dialogue and friendship with Charles Hartshorne, the Ashbel Smith Emeritus Professor of Philosophy at the University of Texas in Austin. What excited me about our conversations and correspondence was Hartshorne's conviction that human beings can attain some knowledge, however infinitesimal, about God. Struggling with issues of faith and belief, my longing for certainty was in tension with my skepticism. Thus, I was fascinated with Hartshorne's rationalistic faith that we can gain some cognitive insight into the divine reality.

What is Hartshorne's background and intellectual preoccupation? Born in 1897, Charles Hartshorne earned his B.A. at Haverford College in 1917, his M.A. at Harvard in 1921, and his Ph.D. at Harvard in 1923. He also studied at the universities of Freiburg and Marburg in Germany. He taught at Harvard, the University of Chicago, and Emory University before joining the faculty of the University of Texas in 1963.

Hartshorne, now ninety-four years of age, is the most persuasive living spokesman of the philosophy of creative process. While at Harvard, he came under the influence of Alfred North Whitehead. With Paul Weiss, he edited for publication the standard edition of the works of Charles Sanders Peirce. Peirce's thought influenced Hartshorne, but deeper and broader than Peirce's influence has been Whitehead's. Hartshorne has affirmed that Whitehead achieved the major metaphysical synthesis of our day,[1] and he has adopted, elaborated, and defended Whiteheadian ideas. Nevertheless, Hartshorne is an original thinker in his own right, and more logically rigorous in his argumentation than Whitehead.

Our concern in this chapter is not the total scope of Hartshorne's thought but rather his philosophical theology—his application of logical analysis to the issues of the nature and existence of God. My concern is with Hartshorne's contribution to the case for God and with an analysis of his conceptuality, utilizing our criteria of consistency, adequacy, and pragmatic value. I am also concerned with the question of the extent to which Hartshorne's process theology is usable by Jewish theologians, both in terms of the doctrine of God and the peculiar and particular theological issues with which Jewish theological thinking grapples in our time.

Reason and the Concept of God

The crux of Hartshorne's analysis of the meaning of "God" involves what he calls "the logic of perfection." Hartshorne is a rationalist; at the early age of seventeen, he reminisces, "After reading Emerson's essays, I made up my mind to trust reason to the end."[2] He explains that a basic conviction of all his writing is expressed in the word *logic*—"the ultimate concepts have a rational structure, lucid, intellectually beautiful."[3] The ultimate concept, for him, is the notion of God, which he considers "the only adequate organizing principle of our life and thought."[4]

A key question then arises. "God" properly denotes the object of worship. But, Hartshorne asks, "Can a worshipful deity be the object of rational analysis or demonstration?"[5] To answer this question, Hartshorne makes use of a principle referred to by philosopher Morris Cohen as the "Law of Polarity." According to this law, Hartshorne explains, "Ultimate contraries are correlatives, mutually interdependent, so that nothing real can be described by the wholly one-sided assertion of simplicity, being, actuality and the like, each in a pure form, devoid and independent of complexity, becoming, potentiality and related contraries."[6]

I have maintained, in the previous chapter, that if there is a God, God's being is complex, for a complex world requires a complex God. Hartshorne's argument on this point is that his logic of perfection requires a complex God. Here Hartshorne is reacting against the classical Thomistic concept of God as *actus purus*, "pure act," which implies a notion of divine perfection as purely simple, actualized, and complete—wholly nonrelative. In contrast to Aquinas, Hartshorne, following Whitehead, argues that perfection is not compromised by richness of experience. Divine perfection need not be synonymous, as Aquinas thought, with simplicity. In fact, Hartshorne maintains, becoming or process (implying that something can be added to the divine experience, that the deity is a growing God) is a more inclusive category than being. How does Hartshorne arrive at this notion that becoming is more inclusive than being?

Hartshorne's argument is that we can conceive of becoming as including being, but being cannot be so conceived that it entirely includes its own contrast with becoming. A novel factor together with an established non-novel factor results in a novel togetherness or creative synthesis of the two factors. Furthermore, to arrive at the factor of pure being, we must abstract from the total concrete reality insofar as it becomes. Becoming, the concrete factor, thus includes being, the abstract factor.[7]

Applying this analysis to God, Hartshorne maintains that God is "the union of...supreme being and supreme becoming."[8] Hartshorne criticizes classical theism for its "monopolar prejudice." Hartshorne is referring to the practice of putting God on only one side, or one pole, of a pair of metaphysical contraries. Thus, according to classical theism, God is absolute, creator, infinite, and necessary, while the world is relative, created, finite, and contingent. Hartshorne maintains that this view is too simple. He holds that God is both absolute and relative, creator and created, infinite and finite, necessary and contingent—in short, the union of supreme being and supreme becoming, or being in the process of becoming. Hartshorne refers to this double predication as the principle of dual transcendence: It takes both sides of metaphysical contraries to characterize God. Thus, Hartshorne envisages God as dipolar: God has a necessary pole and a contingent pole, and absolute aspect and a relative aspect, etc.

Hartshorne's dipolar theology seems vulnerable to the charge of inconsistency and self-contradiction. He attempts to avoid contradictions by distinguishing various aspects of the predication of divine attributes. He maintains, for example, that God is not necessary and contingent in the same respect. Although the divine existence is necessary (otherwise God would not be the ultimate source of explanation), the particular manner in which his existence is actualized is contingent. Hartshorne thus distinguishes divine existence from divine actuality. The fact that God exists is necessary, but that God exists with just the knowledge, feeling, and value that God has is contingent upon the state of the universe at a particular time. Thus, there is potency in God in the sense that God grows with the world; God has an infinite capacity to adjust to any world-state that becomes actual.

Does Hartshorne in fact avoid contradiction on this point? This question is crucial, especially for Hartshorne, with his avowed allegiance to reason. Hartshorne does not see any contradiction involved in ascribing opposing metaphysical categories to the same reality provided they refer to different aspects of that reality. According to Hartshorne, the law of noncontradiction is incorrectly formulated as "no subject can have the predicates p and not-p at the same time."[9] What needs to be made clear is that they cannot be applied in the same respect. Thus, a person can change in some respects without changing in every way. The universe keeps changing, yet we can refer to its changeless activity; namely, the fact that it never ceases to change. Similarly, for Hartshorne, God can be regarded as immutable in regard to ultimate purpose but mutable with respect to new specific objectives in response to the created world. God may also be said to exist necessarily in terms of God's essence, but contingently with respect to God's reaction to the world. The upshot of the matter is that the predication of contrasting attributes in God is not on the same ontological level, since one set refers to the concrete aspect of God, the other to the abstract aspect.[10] Hence, Hartshorne is not guilty of contradiction because the contrasting attributes he predicates make reference to differing ontological levels of the divine being.

It may be objected that Hartshorne's intricate analysis of God does away with the sense of mystery that is a necessary component of worship. Hartshorne's reply is that he locates the mystery in God's concrete actuality—God's becoming—to which no concept can do justice. The entire actual God whom we confront in worship—the supreme concrete becoming reality—is for Hartshorne a mystery that transcends our concepts. It is only the abstract essence of God that Hartshorne claims is knowable. Hartshorne explains:

> What we call His essence or His attribute of perfection is the common denominator of God loving this world....One may admit the impenetrable divine

mystery but believe also in the unrivaled lucidity of the divine essence as an abstract aspect of the mystery.[11]

The supreme abstract principle uniquely identifying God's being is, for Hartshorne, the attribute of perfection. Perfection is the character God must have to be worthy of worship. If, in worship, we seek the greater glory of God, this implies that God is capable of being enriched by human values. Thus Hartshorne's logic of perfection, in exact antithesis to that of Aquinas, requires that to be perfect, God must be forever growing, forever potential. The very perfection of God's being is that it is eternally in the process of becoming; since God is all inclusive, the world-process is part of God. God, for Hartshorne, is the universal self-surpassing and self-perfecting individual, underlying the wholeness of the world.

This is not pantheism, since God is not simply identified with the universe. Rather, God is the universal individual who is inclusive of the universe. Hartshorne's notion is known as *panentheism*: The universe is within God; the contingent aspect of God is in process with the universe while the necessary aspect of God transcends the universe as the mind or soul transcends the body.

One may wonder how, on the basis of reason alone, Hartshorne could arrive at such a conceptuality. Here it is important to note that intuition plays a considerable role in Hartshorne's rationalism. He writes:

Basic ideas derive somehow from direct experience or intuition, life as concretely lived. Moreover, it is demonstrable from almost any classical conception of God that He cannot be known in any merely indirect way, by inference only, but must somehow be present in all experience. No theist can without qualification deny the universal immanence of God.[12]

Hartshorne here echoes Whitehead's contention that God is in the world, or nowhere. Now, what is the universal datum of experience, the intuition wherein God is manifest? Hartshorne envisages God as manifested in worship; Hartshorne's logic of perfection is a logic of worship. He defines worship as "the integrating of all one's thoughts and purposes, all valuations and meanings, all perceptions and conceptions."[13] And he sees the necessary correlative to worship as God, conceived of as the universal individual underlying the cosmic wholeness.

Hartshorne assumes that only by experiencing the reality of God can one experience psychic wholeness. It may be objected that one well-integrated atheist would be a counter-example to this argument, but perhaps Hartshorne would reply by suggesting that such an atheist is merely deluding himself or herself in presuming to be an integrated personality.

In any event, we have seen that Hartshorne's use of reason, abetted by intuition, takes him quite far, much farther than most rationalists—in fact, to a panentheistic conception of God. I contend that Hartshorne is quite correct in his criticism of Aquinas' concept of divine simplicity, but his positive doctrine remains to be established. David Hume expressed pointedly the defects of the concept of divine simplicity: "A mind whose acts and sentiments and ideas are not distinct and successive, one that is wholly simple and totally immutable, is a mind which has no thought, no reason, no will, no sentiment, no love, no hatred; or in a word, is no mind at all."[14]

It seems to me, therefore, that if there is a God, the divine nature is complex, not simple.

What is interesting is that Hartshorne would take exception to the first part of my statement—"if there is a God." Hartshorne would argue that once we admit that the existence of God is contingent, we have already given away the case for God. We have seen Hartshorne's elaborate and intricate discussion of his unique conceptuality of the divine complexity. But how does he know that such a complex being exists? In short, we must now inquire what light Hartshorne sheds on the case for God.

Hartshorne and the Case for God

Hartshorne holds that God is "the only adequate organizing principle of our life and thought."[15] The defense of this claim requires the development of a cumulative case for the existence of God.

The British philosopher Basil Mitchell refers to the combining of several theistic arguments as a cumulative case.[16] Bearing in mind the complexity of the concept of God, one can hardly expect a single argument to settle major issues. One strategy for the theist, therefore, is to claim that theism as a world-picture makes more sense of the evidence than any of the available alternatives. Such a cumulative case would be empirical. The problem with an empirical cumulative case is that neither the theist nor the atheist is in a privileged position with respect to the evidence.[17] The nontheist, for example, can point to the existence of apparently pointless suffering as counter-evidence; the theist can bring up the conspicuous sanctity of the saint as evidence. But neither the theist nor the nontheist is in a privileged position to assess the entire weight of evidence in the universe.

Hartshorne puts the cumulative case argument on a different basis when he maintains that the issue of the divine existence "is purely nonempirical. Hence empirical existential proofs in natural theology are bound to be fallacious."[18] What Hartshorne seeks to establish, therefore, is an *a priori* cumulative case for the existence of God.

The obvious starting point for Hartshorne's case is the ontological argument for the existence of God, the one traditional argument that is *a priori*. The ontological argument for the existence of God was first developed by Anselm (1033–1109), archbishop of Canterbury. It is now recognized that there are two forms of this argument. The first form of the argument runs as follows: By the term *God* is meant a being than which none greater can be conceived—a greatest conceivable being. Now, suppose a greatest conceivable being exists only in the mind, as an idea. Then, Anselm argued, it is possible to conceive of a yet greater being that exists in reality as well as in the mind. Thus, it would be a contradiction to suppose that this greatest conceivable being exists only in the mind. Therefore, the greatest conceivable being must exist in reality.

A standard criticism of this form of the argument derives from the modern German philosopher Kant. Kant held that existence is not a predicate or a property that a thing may have or lack, as this first form of the argument assumes. Hartshorne accepts Kant's criticism as applicable to this form of the argument, "For without existence there is nothing to have or to lack properties. An idea or definition attributes properties hypothetically, it says what a thing of a certain sort must be like if there exists such a thing. Hence, existence is not one of the properties in question."[19]

Hartshorne, however, does accept the second form of Anselm's argument. This second argument arose as Anselm's response to a criticism made by Gaunilon, a monk at Marmontiers in France and a contemporary of Anselm. Gaunilon claimed that Anselm's reasoning would lead to absurd conclusions if applied to other fields. Utilizing a parallel ontological argument, Gaunilon asserted, one could ostensibly prove the existence of a most perfect island. Anselm's reply to Gaunilon emphasized the uniqueness of the idea of God, attempting to show that ontological reasoning applies only to this unique idea. In his second form of the argument, Anselm maintained that the element in the idea of God that is lacking in the notion of the most perfect island is necessary existence. An island or any material object is part of the contingent world. Hence, "the most perfect island" can without contradiction be thought of as not existing. Anselm's argument, in its second form, refers to a necessarily existent being, a being that has the ultimate perfection that it cannot be conceived of as not existing.

Reconstructing the second form of Anselm's ontological argument, the version that Hartshorne accepts runs as follows. The premise of the argument is that the concept of God as eternal, self-existent being is such that the question of whether God exists cannot be a contingent question but rather must be one of logical necessity or impossibility. A being that exists, but of whom it is conceivable that being might not have existed, would be less than God. For only a being whose existence is necessary rather than contingent can be that than which nothing greater is conceivable. But if such a necessary being does not exist, it must be a necessary rather than a contingent fact that such a being does not exist. Thus, God's existence is either logically necessary or logically impossible. However, it has not been shown to be impossible—that is, the concept of such a being has not been demonstrated to be impossible. Therefore, we must conclude that God necessarily exists.

Now we can understand why Hartshorne maintains that to say "if God exists, God exists necessarily" is to give the theistic case away. He holds this because a being that exists, but of whom it is conceivable that that being might not have existed, would be less than God. Only a being whose existence is logically necessary can be such that nothing greater can be conceived.

Thus, Hartshorne is of the opinion that if the idea of God is logically possible, then God must exist—namely, if we can conceive of God properly, God's existence is logically necessary. The only alternative to theism, for Hartshorne, is positivism, which denies that God can be coherently conceived.

What can be said about Hartshorne's reconstruction of Anselm's second form of the ontological argument? John Hick criticizes Hartshorne's argument, alleging that it confuses two different concepts of necessary being: logical necessity, and ontological or factual necessity. Hick contends that logical necessity applies only to propositions: A proposition is logically necessary if it is true by virtue of the meanings of the terms composing it. Hick accepts the basic empirical principle that existential propositions cannot be logically necessary: Whether or not a given kind of entity exists is a question of empirical fact and not of the rules of language. Accordingly, Hick interprets Anselm to be referring to ontological necessity that if God exists, God's existence is *a se,* i.e., eternal and independent existence. Thus, it is Hick's contention that while Anselm's argument establishes that the concept of God involves the idea of God's necessary existence in the sense of God's aseity, the argument cannot establish that this concept of an eternally existent being is exemplified in reality.[20]

Hartshorne replies to Hick's objections in his essay "John Hick on Logical and Ontological Necessity."[21] Hartshorne observes that both he and Hick agree that all existence implies God as its creative ground. What Hartshorne questions is whether Hick can really conceive of the divine nonexistence. Hartshorne asks:

> Is it the existence of bare nothing? I take this to be a series of words with no clear, consistent, specifiable meaning. Is it the existence of a godless world? And what would constitute this godlessness? A great amount of evil? How much beyond what the actual world holds?[22]

The burden of Hartshorne's argument is that if we can conceive of God correctly, we must conceive of God's existence as logically necessary. But what is interesting in Hartshorne's reply is his frank admission that he is unsure that he or anyone else can conceive of God correctly. Thus he writes, "All my difficulty in believing in theism, all of it, turns on the not easily disproved suspicion that every available formulation of the idea of God involves some more or less well-hidden absurdity."[23] Thus, this philosopher who would "know" God has his doubts too, but what he doubts is the *a priori* issue of the very conceivability of God. The issue for Hartshorne is the inner coherence of the idea of God. It is for this reason that Hartshorne maintains that if the idea of God is logically possible, then God exists necessarily. Either the idea of God is a genuine idea or a pseudo-idea, a genuine possibility or an impossibility: These are the stark alternatives to Hartshorne. What the ontological argument brings to light, therefore, is the issue of the conceivability of divinity. What, then, is the function of the other arguments for God's existence, according to Hartshorne?

Hartshorne admits that the ontological argument, all by itself, is not a convincing proof. Rather, he contends, there are a number of theistic arguments that reinforce each other:

> The ontological argument has to assume the conceivability of divinity, whereas the other arguments try to show that the inconceivability of divinity implies the inconceivability of other ideas so fundamental and useful that one must at least hope deity is not inconceivable, not implicitly contradictory or hopelessly vague in meaning.[24]

Let us therefore see how Hartshorne develops some of these other arguments. The form of the cosmological argument that Hartshorne utilizes is from contingent to noncontingent being, but he gives it a different twist. Hartshorne's premise is the inconceivability of absolute nonbeing. Hartshorne contends that our conceptual machinery breaks down in trying to explicate the idea of pure nothing.[25] "Something exists" is thus for Hartshorne a necessary truth. Now, since nonbeing is inconceivable and since no individual or group of individuals existing contingently can account for the necessity of existence, therefore, Hartshorne concludes, there must be at least one individual—God—who exists necessarily.

Clearly, Hartshorne's arguments rely heavily on intuition. He admits in this connection that "all proof rests on intuition somewhere."[26] What is interesting is that many theists, in addition to nontheists, would not accept Hartshorne's intuition that "something exists" is a necessary truth. In Hartshorne's metaphysical system, God is not and never was without a world. There is a kind of necessity in creation since God could not have been without some kind of world. For Hartshorne, God does not choose to have a world; God has to have one. Here Hartshorne follows Plato in asserting the inconceivability of a divine being acting without restriction to given conditions, by a world. It follows that Hartshorne views the classical idea of *creatio ex nihilo* as incoherent. Obviously, the classical theist has a competing intuition. The author of the Hebraic hymn "Adon Olam" (Lord of the Universe), articulating the classical view, clearly had no difficulty conceiving of a supreme being without a world as he wrote these lines:

> Lord of the World, He reigned alone
> While yet the universe was naught,
> When by His will all things were wrought,
> Then first His sovereign name was known.[27]

The upshot of the matter is that Hartshorne's argument relies too heavily on his intuition of the inconceivability of pure nothing; others may argue that they can conceive of pure nonbeing. Thus Hartshorne's cosmological argument results in a stalemate, and has force only for those who are willing to accept his *a priori* presuppostion, his intuition.

Hartshorne's *a priori* version of the argument from design rests upon a similar presupposition. His intuition here is that complete cosmic chaos is inconceivable. Hartshorne's statement of the argument is as follows:

> Thus, in the reasonable argument from design, we may argue that if all interaction is supposed to be local and more or less unknowing, it is not to be understood how reality could be or remain anything by a "shapeless chaos"—to quote Jefferson's phrase, used in this connection. Only universal interactions can secure universal order, or impose and maintain laws of nature cosmic in scope and relevant to the past history of the universe. The argument is not observational. For, if this reasoning is correct, the alternative to God's existence is not an existing chaos but, rather, nothing conceivable. The argument is that the very concept of reality (and any significant "unreality" as well) implicitly involves order and an orderer. Apart from God not only would this world not be conceivable, but no

world, and no state of reality, or even of unreality, could be understood.[28]

Hartshorne's argument is that God is an *a priori* necessary ontological presuppostion for the intelligibility of the world. Hartshorne holds that the order of nature is an instance of social order. A universe consisting merely of a plurality of agents unrestricted and unlimited by any universal cosmic laws set up by a supreme agent would be a shapeless chaos. Such a completely unordered universe is inconceivable for Hartshorne; he holds that there is no possibility of complete chaos. Furthermore, only a supreme cosmic agent could secure this cosmic order. Hence God, the one universal individual conceivable *a priori*, must exist.

The problem with Hartshorne's attempt to cast the empirical argument from design into a nonempirical form lies in the fact that any claim to the effect that something is or is not conceivable cannot be divorced from empirical and scientific considerations.[29] For example, the scientist Paul Davies suggests that "it is unnecessary to suppose that the universe was created in a remarkably ordered state after all. The primeval material was actually in a state of total disorder (maximum entropy)."[30] Whereas the ontological argument is clearly *a priori*, and it is possible to recast the cosmological argument in *a priori* form if one accepts Hartshorne's intuitions, it simply goes against the grain of the entire thrust of the design argument to recast it in a totally *a priori* form.

However, a combination of Whiteheadian considerations along with Hartshorne's insights can be utilized to strengthen the argument from design. Whitehead at first appealed to the abstract principle of concretion to explain why just this selection of pure possibilities shall be actual in our world order. Later on, he became convinced that more is necessary than an abstract principle, for abstractions cannot do anything by themselves. Principles and laws are merely names for patterns in what we observe. They do nothing. Thus Whitehead came to the conclusion that the agency that accomplishes the concretion must be an actual entity. Hartshorne adds to this consideration the concept that there must be a universal individual who has cosmic scope—a cosmic agent—to set limits to chaos and to shape the order of the cosmos. And if the world is viewed in organic terms, as Whitehead does, the cosmic agent must be immanent in the organic process.

Hartshorne's emphasis on the *a priori* is correct in this respect: There is an *a priori* element in the argument from design, even though the argument as a whole cannot be divorced from scientific and empirical considerations. The *a priori* element is the intuition that cosmic order is not self-explanatory. Here the atheist counters with the competing intuition that whatever order exists in the universe is sheer brute fact, requiring no explanation. I hold with Whitehead and Hartshorne that the deep intuition that the order and complexity of the world require for their explanation an immanent divine ordering entity points to the reality of God. The marvelous, intricate, and dynamic adjustments made by the cells in the human body, for example, seem to point to the existence of a divine orderer. But a deep intuition is not a proof, and I recognize the possibility, argued by atheists and agnostics, that the order is simply a brute fact.

The upshot of the matter is that Hartshorne is correct in noting the importance of *a priori* presuppositions in developing the case for God, but he takes this principle to absurd lengths in denying the relevance of scientific and empirical considerations. In terms of the traditional arguments for the existence of God, therefore, we are left with a stalemate of competing intuitions.

I suggest, therefore, that the case must be shifted from a purely cognitive to a moral plane. This shift should not be surprising, given the current situation in philosophy. Epistemological claims about the foundations of knowledge concerning the external world, let alone the existence of God, are now in question. In this book we have been examining world-pictures. The contemporary philosopher Richard Rorty argues that the history of Western philosophy is dominated by a picture that he calls "the mirror of nature."[31] He explains:

It is pictures rather than propositions, metaphors rather than statements, which determine most of our philosophical convictions. The picture which holds traditional philosophy captive is that of the mind as a great mirror, containing various representations—some accurate, some not—and capable of being studied by pure, nonempirical methods. Without the notion of mind as mirror, the notion of knowledge as accuracy of representation would not have suggested itself.[32]

What Rorty attempts to do is to deconstruct this picture, arguing that the discovery of correspondences between thought or language and the "objective" world must be abandoned, and with it the idea of philosophy as centered in a theory of representation. Philosophy must therefore no longer be thought of as providing a tribunal of pure reason to judge other areas of culture. Rather, the aim of a philosophy without mirrors will be to continue the conversation that constitutes our culture, rather than to pronounce on its results from an ahistorical point of view.

It is beyond the scope of this book to evaluate Rorty's thesis. What does seem to be apparent, however, is that a simple correspondence theory of truth seems no longer tenable, for the very assumption that words "hook into" objects in any simplistic sense seems to be discredited by recent philosophy. On this point, Whitehead is more relevant than Russell. Throughout his philosophical career, Russell assumed that if language is to have meaning, it must correspond, in its terms and syntax, to the ultimate nature of events and the structure of reality.[33] Whitehead was much closer to the contemporary discussion in his belief concerning the incapacity of language to express our deepest thoughts. Although he would not have subscribed to Rorty's deconstruction of the mind as the mirror of nature, he did hold that what the mind can know are only approximations. Thus, in our discussion of the case for God, we have not assumed a correspondence theory of truth. Rather, our criteria have been inner consistency, adequacy to human experience, and pragmatic value.

Now, one suggestion that Rorty makes has a considerable value for this discussion. He states, "Philosophy which was utterly unedifying, utterly irrelevant to such moral choices as whether or not to believe in God would count not as philosophy, but as some special sort of science."[34] What is interesting here is the reference to belief in God as a moral choice.

I have been arguing in this book that the case for the existence of a supernatural God above and beyond the universe has no content because we have no experience of universes. I have maintained that, due to our human cognitive limitations, the case should focus on whether there are factors within the universe that point to the working of a divine agency immanent in our experience of the world. The resulting conclusion to which we have come is that belief or disbelief in an immanent divine actuality depends on the basic presuppostion or presuppositions that constitute the foundation of one's particular worldview. The specific conclusion set forth here is that such a basic presupposition is ultimately a moral choice, a value judgment concerning the world and our place in the universe.

Underlying Bertrand Russell's animus against theism, for example, is his value judgment concerning the inferior character of our universe. Take, for example, this observation by Russell:

> Nor is there, so far as I can see, any particular comfort to be derived from the hypothesis that the world was made by a Creator. Whether it was, or whether it was not, it is what it is. If somebody tried to sell you a bottle of very nasty wine, you would not like it any better for being told that it had been made in a laboratory and not from the juice of the grape. In like manner, I see no comfort to be derived from the supposition that this very unpleasing universe was manufactured of set purpose.[35]

In contrast, one of Hartshorne's basic presuppositions is the idea of God as the loving, all-inclusive, cosmic individual who constitutes the universe as an integral whole, and that human beings can attain wholeness or integrity only by worshiping God. Hartshorne maintains that this presupposition can be stated as an argument. He calls it the "religious or global" proof, because "it sums up all the others." He also refers to it as an argument from "the essential religious value" as constituting "the very meaning of life."[36] He sees it as comparable to William James' notion of the will to believe and Kant's primacy of the practical will, while adding theoretical considerations to their moral arguments.[37]

Hartshorne characterizes his argument as stemming from the rational necessity of religious experience and of God as its adequate referent. He explains:

> If an individual must have integrity in order to exist as an individual, and if the conscious form of integrity is worship, then while an individual may live by unconscious integrity, or may to some extent lack integrity, he cannot consciously and rationally choose to do either of these. Hence there is something irrational in choosing not to believe in God. There seems no other way than the theistic to conceive the objective correlate of personal integrity. How can various interests form one complex interest, various loves one complex love, unless the totality of objects of interest or love is felt to constitute a reality at least as unified or integrated as the creaturely individual?[38]

The first point to notice is that Hartshorne characterizes worship as the conscious form of integrity. Hartshorne, we recall, defined worship as "the integrating of all one's thoughts and purposes, all valuations and meanings, all perceptions and conceptions."[39] What Hartshorne's argument amounts to is the claim that the human individual can be fully integrated only insofar as he or she responds to the integrity of the cosmos—i.e., the cosmos as unified by God as the universal individual. The atheist or agnostic lives either in unconscious integrity or simply lacks integrity—despite, Hartshorne would argue, any of his disclaimers. Essentially, the core of Hartshorne's argument is his view of the inadequacy of humanism as a worldview. In *Beyond Humanism*, Hartshorne writes:

Humanism condemns us to a lack of integration within knowledge itself. For just as God is nature as infinitely lovable, so he is nature as infinitely intelligible. To say nature is godless is to say that it is not basically intelligible. The only thing that fully explains itself to a purposive rational mind is a purposive rational mind; everything else suggests the need for explanation.[40]

Hartshorne's antihumanistic argument thus glides into the teleological argument for a divine purposive mind. Are we, then, morally justified in believing in a divine purposive mind?

The issue here involves the ethics of belief debate. W.K. Clifford and others, including Bertrand Russell, hold that we are never justified in believing anything that is not strictly in accord with the evidence. In contrast, in his essay "The Will to Believe," William James held that "our passional nature not only may, but must, decide an option between propositions, whenever it is a genuine option that cannot by its nature be decided on intellectual grounds."[41] For to remain in indecision, James asserted, is to risk losing the truth. In other words, by "willing to believe" in God, we open ourselves to aspects of reality—its beauty, orderliness, creativity as manifestations of the divine—that we would not experience otherwise.

Where Hartshorne differs from James is that he would not draw such a sharp line of demarcation between passional and intellectual beliefs. It is precisely Hartshorne's point that to attain personal harmony and integrity, a unity of our intellectual and passional natures, we need to worship God as the objective correlate of our human integrity. God thus represents for Hartshorne the integrity of the universe, its ultimate intelligibility. Hartshorne's notion here is similar to that of William E. Hocking with whom he studied, namely, that God represents the notion that we are not alone in knowing the world, and the faith that those aspects of the universe we do not know are known by God. "I know not; but He knows"[42]—only this claim can give the universe an integrity to which we are responding when we seek to be whole.

The conclusion of this section is that Hartshorne clarifies the nature of the case for God. A case for God is based on the basic ontological presupposition of the ultimate intelligibility and integrity of the universe, manifesting the existence of a universal individual or cosmic agent. This being is the ground of order, novelty, value, and unity. Hartshorne's attempt to spell out this insight in terms of formal proofs is successful only for those who are willing to accept his basic intuitions as premises for these arguments. What Hartshorne does succeed in showing is that the believer is morally justified in the act of belief that the search for personal self-integration has as its objective correlate the divine integrity of the universe.

Here the believer may respond to the nonbeliever: "I need this belief to attain my own personal self-integration. You are free to seek self-integration in other ways, but you cannot ask me to wait until all the evidence is in, because neither you nor I am in a privileged position with respect to all the evidence in the universe." By the same token, the skeptic has the right to object to Hartshorne's assumption that somehow the skeptic is unconsciously religious or lacks self-integration. Just as the believer is morally justified in believing, so the skeptic is morally justified in not believing.

Ultimately, the issue of belief or disbelief in God is a personal choice based on each individual's interpretation of the available evidence. My personal choice is for belief in God illuminated by the insights of process theology, but I am tolerant of and understand the skeptic's hesitation because of the skeptical side of my own nature. My response to the nonbeliever and the searching skeptic is: "Become more aware of your own presuppositions, and of religious alternatives such as process theology—and, hopefully, become more open thereby to the possibility of belief in the reality of God."

Evaluation of Hartshorne's Philosophical Theology

The problem of the inner consistency of Hartshorne's philosophical theology arises with respect to his dipolar concept of God as the union of being and becoming. We have seen that Hartshorne avoids contradiction by explaining that his ascription of opposing metaphysical categories to the same reality refers to different aspects or ontological levels of God. If one accepts the notion of God's being as complex, in direct antithesis to Aquinas' concept of the divine simplicity, then one can also accept Hartshorne's predication of differing ontological levels in God.

It may be asked how the Jewish theologian might react to Hartshorne's idea of the divine dipolarity and complexity. A simplistic answer would claim that Judaism asserts the unknowability of the divine essence ("Man may not see Me and live" [Exodus 33:20]). However, closer inspection of Jewish sources reveals an entire stream of Jewish tradition, the Kabbalistic or mystical, that emphasizes the inner life of God. A.J. Heschel, a leading interpreter of Jewish mysticism, states, "The concept of the inner life of the Divine Being is an idea upon which the mystic doctrines of Judaism hinge."[43] Heschel further explains that one of the boldest ideas of Jewish mysticism is that "not only is God necessary to man but that man is also necessary to God, to the unfolding of His plans in the world."[44] The notion that we human beings can add to the glory of God and contribute to the inner divine life is quite in consonance with Jewish mysticism.

With respect to the criterion of adequacy to the full range of human experience, Hartshorne surely does evaluate the idea of God from many diverse standpoints. Hartshorne is particularly sensitive to the problem of evil. Like Whitehead, he finds the notion of divine omnipotence a morally outrageous notion. He adds to Whitehead's critique of divine omnipotence his own contention that the notion is incoherent. Hartshorne's argument for this view is that the notion of a cosmic power that could determine all decisions fails to make sense, because the very notion of a "world" implies local agents making their own decisions. Hartshorne is not merely saying that God's power is limited. Rather, he is asserting that God's power is absolutely maximal, but the greatest possible power is still one power among others and is not the only power.

God, then, for Hartshorne, is the universal cosmic agent who possesses adequacy of cosmic power—the power to do for the cosmos all the desirable things that could be done or need be done. A major function of God, Hartshorne contends, is to set limits to chance, to provide a favorable ratio of risk and opportunity. Chance cannot be all pervasive because then there would be complete chaos, no world at all. But a world totally without chance is also inconceivable for Hartshorne. "A world without risks," Hartshorne writes, "is not conceivable."[45] In support of this contention, Hartshorne adduces a new idea discovered in contemporary physics that "causal order is not absolute but statistical. It admits an element of chance or randomness in nature."[46]

What Hartshorne is saying is that God's plan for the world is indeterminate in its details. Otherwise, the world process would be an idle duplicate of an eternal plan. This notion of real novelty and creative process in the world gives rise to Hartshorne's ethics of belief, which is of particular relevance to Jewish theological belief after the Holocaust:

> The properly constituted man does not want to rely upon God to arrange all things, including our own decisions, in accordance with a plan of events which fixes every last detail with reference to every other that ever has happened or ever is to happen....God is to be relied upon to do for the world all that ought to be done for it, and with as much survey of the future as there ought to be, or as is ideally desirable, leaving for the members of the community to do for themselves and each other all that ought to be left to do.[47]

Excessive or extravagant expectations are the prelude to disappointment and despair. Jewish post-Holocaust despair is a consequence of expecting too much from God, an expectation deriving from the biblical picture of the intervening or interruptive God. Hartshorne's notion of a deity who has adequate cosmic power, a cosmic agent who sets up the ratio of risk and opportunity and who limits change through the laws of nature, seems to be a more realistic notion of God for our time. From the point of view of adequacy, it therefore appears that Hartshorne's philosophical theology speaks especially to those in our time who have experienced the absence of miraculous divine intervention but who still seek to commune with God.

But—and this is the issue of pragmatic value—why seek to commune at all with Hartshorne's God? What practical effect, what value for living, can be found in this philosophical theology? We have seen that one value is the integration of the self. But is this enough? What does Hartshorne's God do for the individual?

Hartshorne's panentheism—the worldview that God includes but is "more" than the world—is the concept of the deity as the supreme world-mind: "The inclusiveness of the world-mind," Hartshorne writes, "means, not that it is exalted above all suffering, but that no pain and no joy is beneath its motive. All things make their immediate contribution to the one, but they contribute what they are and have, their sorrow as well as their joy."[48] Hartshorne's notion provides a meaning to life, one especially in accord with Jewish religious teachings. Hartshorne has Judaism in mind when he speaks of the meaning of human life as the wish "to contribute every experience...to the One who alone is capable of accepting the gift in its fullness—the Holy One, Blessed be He."[49] ("The Holy One, Blessed be He" is a Jewish rabbinic name of God.)

However, one may ask whether Hartshorne's God, who suffers with us and feels our pain but who cannot or does not intervene to stop it, is worthy of worship. Hartshorne is on the horns of the old dilemma:

The more God is like one of us, needs his creatures and is unable to prevent evil and suffering in the short or long term, the less he seems worthy of worship—he might be worthy of sympathy rather more. On the other hand, if God is all-powerful, it seems monstrous that he should use the suffering of others to perfect himself. If he can stop it at all, why does he stop it now? The proper response to such a being would hardly be one of worship.[50]

Hartshorne's God is an infinitely self-surpassing, self-perfecting God. But such a God is not all powerful. So the second horn of the dilemma does not apply. What of the first horn of the dilemma? Is Hartshorne's "Suffering God" more worthy of sympathy than worship? The question is crucial.

To deal with this issue, I draw an analogy from a suicide prevention group known as the Samaritans. The Samaritans listen to the caller but do not offer advice. The Samaritan philosophy, based on respect and tolerance for others, is known as befriending. Its prominent feature is patience. Chad Verrah, the Samaritans' founder, unpacks the meaning of this word: "The word 'patience' is derived from the Latin word for suffering, and those who would befriend the suicidal are in fact those who are willing to suffer, and suffer with, fellow human beings."[51]

If, in fact, God does suffer with God's creatures (and this notion is found in Jewish sources—e.g., "I will be with him in trouble [Psalm 91:15]—as well as in the Christian tradition), this would indeed be a worshipful attribute of the deity. Moreover, Hartshorne would say that a constantly intervening deity would violate the autonomy of nature and human freedom. So the first horn of the dilemma is not an insuperable difficulty for Hartshorne.

But a basic objection underlying this dilemma remains, namely, is Hartshorne's notion of God too anthropomorphic? Hartshorne's reply to this is to quote Goethe's dictum that "all thought is anthropomorphic." To refer to God as a "force," for example, is anthropomorphic for the only usage we know of this term is "our usage." Moreover, we are removing the term *force* from its usual habitat, physics, and placing it in a religious context where it has no clear meaning.

My intuition on this point is that Hartshorne is so concerned to say something "meaningful" about God that some of the mystery of the divine is lost (although Hartshorne does locate the mystery in the divine actuality). But this loss of the sense of divine transcendence is a consequence of engaging in philosophical debate with those who regard the recourse to mystery as (to use the Spinozistic phrase) the asylum of ignorance. I have stressed the divine immanence precisely for this reason. But the authentic religious view is that God is both transcendent and immanent, as the prophet Isaiah wrote, "Holy, holy, holy is the Lord of hosts, the whole earth is full of His glory" (Isaiah 6:3). Holy in this context means "transcendent." To the skeptical philosopher, "transcendent" is a question-begging term; to the religious believer, it beckons to an unseen mysterious reality.

Hartshorne's panentheism, the view that God includes but is "more than" the world, implies that we are like cells in the divine organism. The idea is that just as we are "immanent" in our own bodies, so God is immanent in us, but God transcends us as we transcend our own cells. A profound reflection on God was that of a biologist who remarked to me, "As we are to the amoeba, so God is to us." Loren Eiseley, the anthropologist, expressed a similar thought:

> So relative is the cosmos we inhabit that, as we gaze upon the outer galaxies available to the reach of our telescopes, we are placed in about the position that a single white blood cell in our bodies would occupy, if it were intelligently capable of seeking to understand the nature of its own universe, the body it inhabits....It could never know there was an outside, a vast being on a scale it could not conceive of and of which it formed an infinitesimal part.[52]

Here is the essential religious insight. We are fragments of the divine, part of a larger whole, individuations of the divine spirit. The divine actuality is the immanent aspect of the divine, the divine process of which we are parts, God as consequent. The necessary existence of God, God's immutable essence, is God as stasis, the divine inner core, God as primordial. The mystery is the unity of the primordial and consequent natures, the union of divine existence and the divine actuality. The mystery of this unity is paralleled by the search for our own inner unity of self, since we as God's creatures are aspects of being in the process of becoming.

Notes

[1]Charles Hartshorne, "The Compound Individual," *Philosophical Essays for Alfred North Whitehead*. Longmans, Green and Co., 1936, p. 212.

[2]Hartshorne, *The Logic of Perfection*. The Open Court Publishing Co., 1926, p. viii.

[3]*Ibid.*, p. ix.

[4]*Ibid.*, p. xix.

[5]*Ibid.*, p. 3f.

[6]Charles Hartshorne and William L. Reese, eds., *Philosophers Speak of God*. University of Chicago Press, 1953, p. 2.

[7]Hartshorne in *Philosophical Interrogation*, edited with an Introduction by Sydney and Beatrice Rome. Holt, Rinehart and Winston, p. 321. See also Hartshorne's *Creative Synthesis and Philosophic Method*. The Open Court Publishing Co., 1970.

[8]Hartshorne and Reese, *Philosophers Speak of God*, p. 14.

[9]Santiago Sia, *God in Process Thought*. Martinus Nijhoff Publishers, 1985, p. 49.

[10]*Ibid.*, pp. 43, 49.

[11]Hartshorne, *The Logic of Perfection*, p. 4f.

[12]Charles Hartshorne, *A Natural Theology for Our Time*. The Open Court Paperback, 1967, p. 2.

[13]*Ibid.*, p. 4f.

[14]David Hume, *Dialogues Concerning Natural Religion*, edited with an Introduction by Henry D. Acken. Hafner Publishing Co., 1943, p. 32.

[15]Hartshorne, *The Logic of Perfection*, p. xix.

[16]See Basil Mitchell, *The Justification of Religious Belief*. Oxford University Press, 1981, p. 39ff.

[17]See Donald Wayne Viney, *Charles Hartshorne and the Existence of God.* State University of New York Press, 1985, p. 7.

[18]Hartshorne, *A Natural Theology for Our Time,* p. 53.

[19]Charles Hartshorne, "What Did Anselm Discover" in *The Many-Faced Argument,* edited by John Hick and Arthur McGill. The Macmillan Co., 1967, p. 322.

[20]John Hick, "The Ontological Argument for the Existence of God" in *The Encyclopedia of Philosophy,* edited by Paul Edwards. The Macmillan Co., 1967, Vol. 5, pp. 538–542.

[21]Charles Hartshorne, "John Hick on Logical and Ontological Necessity," *Religious Studies* 13, pp. 155–165.

[22]*Ibid.,* p. 158.

[23]*Ibid.,* p. 156.

[24]*Ibid.,* p. 164f.

[25]Charles Hartshorne, "Could There Have Been Nothing? A Reply," *Process Studies* I (Spring 1971), p. 25.

[26]*Ibid.,* p. 27.

[27]*Weekday Prayer Book.* Rabbinical Assembly, 1974, p. 5.

[28]Hartshorne, *A Natural Theology for Our Time,* p. 53.

[29]See Viney, p. 141.

[30]Paul Davies, *God and the New Physics.* Simon and Schuster, 1983, p. 176.

[31]Richard Rorty, *Philosophy and the Mirror of Nature.* Princeton University Press, 1979.

[32]*Ibid.,* p. 12.

[33]Morris Weitz, review of Bertrand Russell's *My Philosophical Development* in *The Philosophical Review,* January 1961, p. 113.

[34]*Ibid.,* p. 384.

[35]Bertrand Russell, *The Scientific Outlook.* W.W. Norton and Co., 1962, p. 118.

[36]Hartshorne, *A Natural Theology for Our Time,* p. 45.

[37]*Ibid.,* p. 47f.

[38]*Ibid.,* p. 45f.

[39]*Ibid.,* p. 4f.

[40]Charles Hartshorne, *Beyond Humanism.* University of Nebraska Press, 1937, p. 23.

[41]William James, "The Will to Believe," 1896, reprinted in Samuel E. Stumpf, *Elements of Philosophy.* McGraw-Hill Co., 1986, p. 277.

[42]William E. Hocking, *The Meaning of God in Human Experience.* Yale University Press, 1912, p. 237.

[43]Abraham J. Heschel, "The Mystical Element in Judaism" in *The Jews: Their History, Culture and Religion,* Vol. II. Jewish Publication Society, 1960, p. 950.

[44]*Ibid.,* p. 934.

[45]Charles Hartshorne, *Omnipotence and Other Theological Mistakes.* State University of New York Press, 1984, p. 12.

[46]*Ibid.,* p. 16.

106   The Case for God

[47]Hartshorne, *The Divine Relativity*. Yale University Press, 1948, p. 24.

[48]Hartshorne, *Logic of Perfection*, p. 202f.

[49]*Ibid.*, p. 243.

[50]Anthony O'Hear, *Experience, Explanation and Faith*. Routledge and Kegan Paul, 1984, p. 198.

[51]Chad Varah, *The Samaritans: Befriending the Suicidal*. Constable and Co., 1980, p. 35.

[52]Loren Eiseley, *The Invisible Pyramid*. Charles Scribner's Sons, 1970, p. 33.